YORK NOTES

D0294283

THE FRENCH LIEUTENANT'S WOMAN

JOHN FOWLES

NOTES BY MICHAEL DUFFY

 Longman

 York Press

The right of Michael Duffy to be identified as Author
of this Work has been asserted by him in accordance
with the Copyright, Designs and Patents Act 1988

YORK PRESS
322 Old Brompton Road, London SW5 9JH

PEARSON EDUCATION LIMITED
Edinburgh Gate, Harlow,
Essex CM20 2JE, United Kingdom
Associated companies, branches and representatives throughout the world

First published 2009

10 9 8 7 6 5 4 3 2 1

ISBN 978–1–4082–1728–3

Phototypeset by Chat Noir Design, France
Printed in China

CONTENTS

PART FIVE
BACKGROUND

PART ONE

INTRODUCTION

STUDYING NOVELS

Reading novels and exploring them critically can be approached in a number of ways, but when reading the text for the first time it is a good idea to consider some, or all, of the following:

- **Format and style**: how do novels differ from other genres? How are chapters or other divisions used to reveal information? Is there a narrator, and if so, how does he or she convey both his or her emotions and those of the characters?

- **The writer's perspective**: consider what the writer has to say, how he or she presents a particular view of people, the world, society, ideas, issues, etc. Are, or were, these views controversial?

- **Shape and structure**: explore how the **narrative** of the story develops – the moments of revelation and reflection, openings and endings, conflicts and resolutions. Is there one main plot or are there multiple plots and sub-plots?

- **Setting**: where and when is the novel set? How do the locations shape or reflect the lives and relationships of the characters? What does the setting add in terms of tone?

- **Choice of language**: does the writer choose to write formally or informally? Does he or she use different registers for characters and narrators, and employ language features such as **imagery** and **dialect**?

- **Links and connections**: what other texts does this novel remind you of? Can you see connections between its narrative, characters and ideas and those of other texts you have studied? Is the novel part of a literary tradition or movement?

- **Your perspective and that of others**: what are your feelings about the novel? Can you relate to the narrators, characters, themes and ideas? What do others say about it – for example, critics, or other writers?

These York Notes offer an introduction to *The French Lieutenant's Woman* and cannot substitute for close reading of the text and the study of secondary sources.

CHECK THE BOOK

For a survey of critical approaches to John Fowles (up to 1990), try the section 'Critical Approaches to the Fiction' in *John Fowles: A Reference Companion* by James R. Aubrey (1991).

READING *THE FRENCH LIEUTENANT'S WOMAN*

READING *THE FRENCH LIEUTENANT'S WOMAN*

CHECK THE BOOK

In the much-quoted 'Notes on an Unfinished Novel', John Fowles says about writing *The French Lieutenant's Woman*, 'I write memoranda to myself about the book I'm on. On this one: *You are not trying to write something one of the Victorian novelists forgot to write; but perhaps something one of them failed to write.* And: *Remember the etymology of the word. A novel is something new: It must have relevance to the writer's now – so don't ever pretend you live in 1867; or make sure the reader knows it's a pretence.*'

The French Lieutenant's Woman, the third of John Fowles's novels, was an immediate success and established his position as a major figure in the mid twentieth-century literary scene. Its success in the critical field is due to its many literary qualities and the many interpretations it invites. However, its initial success probably owes more to those readers who enjoyed an intriguing, romantic adventure in wonderfully evoked settings. Robert Huffaker suggests:

> At its most elementary level, *The French Lieutenant's Woman* is a magnificent historical novel. It is the story of a Dorset farm girl whose strange revolt against Victorian convention frees her for a womanhood among the Pre-Raphaelites in London, while toppling an intelligent young gentleman from the upper class into exile. (*John Fowles*, 1980)

As a Victorian **narrative** written from a twentieth-century perspective, it does not just recreate the England of 1867; nor does it seek to recreate a Victorian novel. What we have instead, besides the strong storyline, is an experimental novel that explores mid Victorian characters and attitudes from the perspective of 1967 with all that the intervening years have revealed in terms of science, religion, politics, social conditions and, of course, literature.

From the very first chapter, the alert reader will notice that the conventions of Victorian fiction are refracted from a twentieth-century perspective, not only in the **allusions** but also in the **voice** (see **Narrative technique and language**). The overt allusions include references to novelists, poets, essayists, scientists, naturalists and political, economic and social theorists, men and women who not only helped to define the Victorian age but also played a part in shaping John Fowles's generation, and beyond it to our own. The references are not confined to those early Victorian figures. Since Fowles does not hide the fact that he is writing from the 1960s, he includes similar references from the one hundred years that separate his narrative and his own times.

The technique Fowles adopts of looking back one hundred years from the present time of writing to the past time of the action of the main narrative involves a number of narrative features – adaptation, imitation, **parody**, **pastiche**, deliberate **anachronistic** juxtapositions and comment, intrusions. Through these Fowles explores many of the central narrative and thematic concerns of the Victorian period – romance, changing social structures, the role of women in a changing society, the emergence of challenging scientific theories, the role of the omniscient author, the use of epigraphs that reflect on the substance of chapters, extracts from the writings of others, and authorial intrusion on a grand scale.

What may be termed the filmic or cinematographic qualities of the novel are a noticeable feature, as they are in so many Victorian novels. The opening chapter, with its panoramic views and close-ups in a dramatic setting, invites the reader to create the scene. Such moments occur frequently throughout the book.

The double perspective of time within the narrative provides various lines of investigation into the structure of the novel. Furthermore, within the narrative Fowles will often move forward and backward in time to challenge the reader in interpreting character or in assessing ideas from different perspectives. When we see Charles rather diffidently considering his future marriage to Ernestina, we have already witnessed his conversation with his uncle in which he has said that he has not yet found the right girl. Added to this is the sense that Sarah, the French lieutenant's woman, seems to have affected him in some way yet to be fully revealed. Fowles has caused the reader to think about character, plot development and narrative technique early in the novel.

As well as clearly signalled references from a range of literary, scientific, historical, political and philosophical sources, the novel is rich in allusions that are woven into the fabric of the text. Fowles, in an interview with Dianne Vipond, said:

> I adore language, and especially English with its incomparable richness. I think of that richness less as a doomed attempt to

CHECK THE FILM

The film of *The French Lieutenant's Woman*, released in 1981, is widely available on DVD. It highlights some interesting problems about transposing the novel to film. One critic, Roger Ebert, said, 'If you see the movie, the book will still surprise you, and that's as it should be' (quoted in *Halliwell's Film Guide*, 8th edition, 1991).

CHECK THE BOOK

For a thought-provoking consideration of Time in *The French Lieutenant's Woman* as well as in Fowles's fiction as a whole, H. W. Fawkner's *The Timescapes of John Fowles* (1984) is recommended reading. Fowles himself approved of this critique and contributed a foreword to the book.

CHECK THE NET

There are many sites that offer interviews with John Fowles. Try the John Fowles website at **www.fowlesbooks.com**, which includes an audio interview with Don Swaim.

CHECK THE BOOK

Thomas C. Foster states that Fowles 'is so good a storyteller, in fact, that readers may be caught up to the extent that they believe the story to be, like its Victorian forebears, the entirety of the novel. One cannot, however, in good conscience write an 1867 novel in 1967 ... too much has changed – in our world view, in our understanding of literature, in our society, in our theology – to continue with narrative in the manner of James or Hardy' (*Understanding John Fowles*, 1994, p. 87).

impose order on chaos than as an attempt to magnify reality. (*Wormholes*, 1998, p. 368)

Fowles's interest in words *per se* is complemented by wide reading in a variety of fiction and non-fiction that finds its way into the novel. Making notes of these patterns of reference will enhance your understanding of the novel's structure and your enjoyment of the writing.

Already aware that the narrator is prepared to break the illusion of fiction by interpolating twentieth-century references and language into the Victorian context, the reader is perhaps a little surprised nevertheless when the author literally stops the action of the narrative, adopts another **voice** and says he is unable to answer the questions he has posed at the end of Chapter 12 ('Who is Sarah? Out of what shadows does she come?', p. 96). He then addresses the reader directly in Chapter 13, simultaneously asserting his authorship and admitting that he cannot control his characters, who have a freedom of their own beyond the control of a God-like omniscient author. However, despite this step into what may be termed **metafiction**, Fowles then resumes the narrative by claiming that he is only reporting the outward facts (p. 99). This is also open to question as he shows that he is willing to impose ideas onto his characters, in this case onto Sarah at the end of Chapter 13.

The puzzling question of the relationship between character, narrator and author is posed by Fowles directly in the novel. On page 97 he openly offers the reader several possibilities: Perhaps I am writing a transposed biography? Perhaps I now live in one of the houses I have brought into the fiction? Perhaps Charles is myself in disguise? Perhaps it is only a game? Perhaps I am trying to pass off a concealed book of essays on you?

These possibilities are part of the games Fowles is playing in the narrative, and while there may be an element of truth in all of them, Fowles has his tongue firmly in his cheek. He gives the reader freedom to interpret the novel in many ways, and each path that may be taken will open up avenues of exploration in the text that are not mutually exclusive or contradictory. Fowles comments on the writing of *The French Lieutenant's Woman* in the context of the 1960s: 'I live in the age of Alain Robbe-Grillet and Roland Barthes; if this is a novel, it cannot be a novel in the modern sense of the word.' There are many moments in the novel when the reader is challenged to use this freedom, never more so than in the closing chapters when, having provided a false ending in Chapter 44, Fowles offers two possible endings to the story.

The density of the text makes it fascinating for students. When asked by Dianne Vipond how he felt about his novels being taught in English classes, Fowles jokingly replied that he felt 'a great deal of pity for the poor devils'. However, he immediately qualified this by adding, 'I believe the literary process is fundamentally beneficial, both for its artists and for its audiences, and especially when it widens their concept of freedom, both personal and social' ('An Unholy Inquisition', John Fowles and Dianne Vipond, reproduced in *Wormholes*, pp. 367–84). It is with this thought foremost in mind that you should approach the novel.

Fowles, probably not exactly out of sympathy for the 'poor devils' referred to above, has left abundant writings, diary entries, interviews and critical commentaries to provide the student with evidence for following individual readings of the text. Moreover, there are many excellent critical works on John Fowles with specific chapters on *The French Lieutenant's Woman* that will help you develop and crystallise your own opinions. These books and articles are referred to throughout the Notes and are detailed in **Further reading**.

Charles Smithson is shown in the story to be undertaking a journey or quest – emotional, social and psychological. This is perhaps the spirit in which the reader should enter this novel. Enjoy the 'magnificent historical novel', the suspense of an erotic romance. Consider evolution in its many senses – that of the individual, of society, of attitudes and beliefs, of authorial position. Explore at the same time the essential questions of freedom at its heart, which apply to author, narrator, character and reader. Take part in the games that Fowles delights in playing on the characters, on the reader and, in self-**parody**, on himself. Examine, as Fowles asks you

---

CONTEXT

Alain Robbe-Grillet (1922–2008), an unorthodox post-modernist French novelist, was a leading figure in the *nouveau roman* group, which flourished from the mid 1950s to the 1960s. Roland Barthes (1915–80) was a French writer and structuralist critic.

CONTEXT

The idea of the quest, undertaken by the hero to find the *princesse lointaine* – the elusive, archetypically unattainable female – has featured in literature in many forms. Fowles acknowledges the influence of Alain-Fournier's *Le Grand Meaulnes* (published in English as *The Lost Domain*).

CONTEXT

In the late twentieth century many writers have examined the relationship between history and the evolution of narrative technique. Novels set in the past but written from a modern perspective include Peter Ackroyd's *The Last Testament of Oscar Wilde* (1983), *Chatterton* (1987) and *Hawksmoor* (1985), and A. S. Byatt's *Possession* (1990).

to, your position as a participant in the novel. In following these paths, you will be following in the wake of millions of readers who have found *The French Lieutenant's Woman* such an intriguing story. There are several critiques, notably from American academics, that will guide you in formulating your own ideas about the characters, themes and narrative techniques in the novel. Remember that when the path forks, as it does for Charles in the novel, you must make your choice based on what you have read in and about the novel. In doing this you will be evolving as a critic yourself, and, as Fowles suggests, as a person.

PART TWO

THE TEXT

NOTE ON THE TEXT

The French Lieutenant's Woman is the most famous and most successful of John Fowles's novels. It has won both popular and critical acclaim in this country and also notably in the United States. The novel was published in 1969. The edition used in these Notes is the paperback reprint published by Vintage in 2004.

SYNOPSIS

Charles Smithson strolls on the Cobb at Lyme Regis with his fiancée, Ernestina Freeman, who is visiting her aunt, Mrs Tranter. It is late March 1867. They see a woman, alone, staring out to sea, and Ernestina reveals her story. The woman is as an outcast from Lyme society. Gossip suggests that she was abandoned by a shipwrecked French sailor, who promised marriage but deserted her after what was seen as an improper encounter. Charles approaches the woman, but is silenced by her piercing look. The woman, Sarah Woodruff, has been taken in by Mrs Poulteney, whose motives are selfish.

We are introduced to Sam Farrer, Charles's servant, who shows interest in Mary, Mrs Tranter's maid.

Charles goes to the Undercliff, an area of Ware Commons rich in fossils. He stumbles across Sarah, who is sleeping on a ledge in the rocks. She wakens suddenly, and after a hasty apology Charles leaves. Later Charles catches up with Sarah on the path back to town. She begs him not to disclose their meeting, as she has been forbidden to walk there.

Ernestina's family background is outlined. Her courtship and engagement are seen in the light of Victorian conventions. This account is followed by a chapter that offers direct comment on authorship and the freedom of characters. Sarah, meanwhile, continues to visit Ware Commons.

> **CONTEXT**
>
> Fowles describes the image that had come to him in a half-sleeping, half-awake state: 'A woman stands at the end of a deserted quay and stares out to sea. … The woman had no face, no particular degree of sexuality. But she was Victorian; and since I always saw her in the same static long shot, with her back turned, she represented a reproach on the Victorian age' ('Notes on an Unfinished Novel' (1969), in *Wormholes*, p. 13).

CHECK THE BOOK
H. W. Fawkner suggests that 'the title of the novel also refers to a French lieutenant's woman in the real world, a certain Marie de Morell, who was unhappily in love with Lieutenant Émile de La Roncière, and who in regular fits of conscious hysteria forged sadistic letters that she claimed were written by the lieutenant' (*The Timescapes of John Fowles*, p. 57).

Charles, Ernestina and Aunt Tranter visit Mrs Poulteney. Charles and Aunt Tranter support the relationship of Sam and Mary, while Ernestina appears rather bigoted. There is a glance of understanding between Charles and Sarah.

Charles and Ernestina are reconciled after their disagreement over Sam and Mary's relationship. Charles believes that he is able to communicate with Sarah, but when they next meet she refuses his assistance. Charles is puzzled as to why she stays in Lyme. He compares Sarah with Ernestina, who now seems shallow to him.

Sarah requests a meeting with Charles on Ware Commons. She gives him two fossils. She asks for another meeting so that she can tell him more of her involvement with Varguennes, the French lieutenant. Charles is aware of the danger of scandal. However, his fascination with Sarah causes him to take the risk of meeting her again.

The local doctor, Dr Grogan, warns Charles of the dangers presented by women suffering from 'melancholia'.

In a further meeting with Charles, Sarah speaks of the lieutenant, who had proposed marriage before seducing her, though she admits that she gave herself freely. She has chosen her role as an outcast to free herself from the need to conform to society. As Sarah and Charles are leaving their secluded meeting place, they see Sam and Mary embracing in the clearing. Sarah smiles at Charles, who is shocked.

Charles receives a letter from his uncle. Ernestina makes presumptuous plans for Charles's inheritance. Meanwhile, Sarah is seen on Ware Commons by Mrs Fairley.

Charles visits his uncle at Winsyatt and learns that he intends to marry a widow who is young enough to bear children, which effectively disinherits Charles from property and title. Charles regrets yet accepts his uncle's decision to marry; Ernestina reacts selfishly to the loss of social standing. Charles is told of Sarah's dismissal and disappearance. A note to Charles from Sarah is seen by Sam, and Sam considers blackmailing his master.

That evening Charles tells Dr Grogan about Sarah's note and his meetings with her. Grogan believes Sarah is luring Charles into a situation that will destroy him. Grogan offers to meet Sarah and arrange a place for her in an asylum. He advises Charles to stay with Ernestina. He gives Charles the transcript of a French court case involving a young lieutenant convicted on the false evidence of a girl. Pages from a medical report tell of another similar case of sexual repression. Charles identifies with the young lieutenant. However, he believes that he can judge Sarah better than Grogan.

Charles finds Sarah sleeping in a barn in the Undercliff. The tension of the situation culminates in their kissing, but Charles then immediately tears himself away. He encounters Sam and Mary on an assignation of their own. Charles tells Sam that this meeting must not be revealed. He advises Sarah to go to Exeter and offers her money. Her last words are that she will never forget him.

Charles creates an excuse to go to London to see Ernestina's father, Mr Freeman. The narrator now breaks the **narrative** with views on Victorian morality.

Sarah settles into a hotel in Exeter. In London Charles meets Ernestina's father, who offers him a position in the family business. Charles feels trapped into a future of commerce and the marriage with Ernestina.

Charles meets two friends at his London club. After a drinking session they visit the Terpsichore, a garish brothel. Charles blunders out in disgust, but he meets a young prostitute. The encounter ends in humiliation as Charles vomits over her pillow when she reveals that her name is Sarah.

A letter from Grogan advises Charles to avoid contact with Sarah and to seek reconciliation with Ernestina. Charles also receives a note, clearly from Sarah, giving him an address. Sam now makes his first moves towards blackmail.

Charles goes to Exeter, accompanied by Sam, who expects that they will stay the night there. However, Charles decides to continue on

CHECK THE BOOK

Carol M. Barnum describes the setting of the encounter between Charles and Sarah: 'The site for the mythic encounter is Ware Commons and its more secret Undercliff, which Fowles invests with the proper aura of strangeness and remoteness, alluding to "its mysteries, its shadows, its dangers" while, at the same time, calling it "an English garden of Eden"' (*The Fiction of John Fowles*, 1988, p. 53).

to Lyme, and he makes a partial confession to Ernestina. There is a contrived Victorian happy ending, with just resolutions for all the characters.

The narrator then insists that this ending was merely in Charles's imagination. The second ending sees Charles return to Exeter to meet Sarah. The encounter in the hotel is carefully stage-managed by Sarah, and eventually they make love. Charles discovers that Sarah had been a virgin. Sarah admits that she lied, and claims that she cannot explain her motives and can never marry him.

Charles goes into a church and struggles with his conscience. He realises that freedom is achieved through the Christian ideals of truth and sincerity. He decides to return to Sarah, after first confessing to Ernestina. Charles writes a letter informing Sarah of his decision, and encloses a brooch.

Sam decides to open the letter and keep the brooch. He tells Charles that there was no answer from Sarah.

Back in Lyme, Charles says he must end the engagement with Ernestina, mentioning a former lover, but not Sarah. Ernestina's attempts to dissuade Charles fail and she turns to anger. She threatens a breach of promise action. When all else fails, she collapses. Grogan guesses that Sarah is the other woman, and cannot believe that Charles could be so easily led into a compromising situation.

On his return to his hotel Charles encounters Sam, who says that he will leave Charles's employment. They part angrily. Mrs Tranter resolves to help Sam and Mary. Grogan cannot accept that Charles and Sarah have any right to a life together. Charles goes to Sarah's hotel, but finds that she has gone, leaving no information. He is furious at discovering from Mrs Endicott and the maid that Sam has deceived him by not delivering the letter. He hopes to find Sarah in London. In the train, the narrator enters the **narrative** as a fellow passenger and watches Charles, trying to determine his fate. He flips a coin to make the decision; Charles looks at the man oddly. At Paddington they go their separate ways.

CHECK THE BOOK

Read the dialogue between Charles's better self and his worse self (pp. 347–9) and about the 'sudden flash of illumination' he experiences as he looks at the Cross. Now read the incident involving Simon and the pig's head on the stick at the end of Chapter 8 of *Lord of the Flies* by William Golding, a writer much admired by Fowles. The inner dialogue and the insights that each character experiences are similar, despite their different contexts.

Charles engages detectives to find Sarah. He receives a summons regarding his broken engagement, but Mr Freeman decides against court action. Charles must sign a declaration of breach of promise, which will be used should he ever decide to marry. Meanwhile Sam, employed by Mr Freeman, is building a relatively prosperous life.

Charles decides to go abroad. He then travels across America, witnessing the aftermath of the American Civil War. In New Orleans a telegram informs him that Sarah has been found.

Charles returns to London to the address that has been anonymously given to him. He finds Sarah living in the house of a Pre-Raphaelite artist. She will not be persuaded to give up her freedom. She tells Charles that there is 'another', which turns out to be a child. Lalage, the daughter that Charles never knew existed, offers the possibility of a happy ending.

The narrator again enters the story. He turns back the clock. Charles is returned to the middle of the conversation fifteen minutes earlier. This time, there is no reconciliation. There is the suggestion of an unmarried relationship, but Charles cannot accept this. Charles believes that he has been deceived all along. However, he finds hope in a new life alone, and an understanding of himself and of endurance in an uncertain world.

DETAILED SUMMARIES

CHAPTERS 1–3

- The Cobb at Lyme Regis is described.
- Charles and Ernestina meet the French lieutenant's woman on the Cobb.
- Ernestina reveals some of the history of the woman.
- Charles, at thirty-two years of age, evaluates his life and his forthcoming marriage.

CHECK THE NET

The Pre-Raphaelite Brotherhood was founded by the English painters John Everett Millais (1829–96) and Dante Gabriel Rossetti (1828–82), among others. See the website of The Pre-Raphaelite Society for more information – **www.pre-raphaelitesociety.org**

CONTEXT

In an article in the *New York Times* on 13 November 1977, John Fowles commented: 'In some ways the unhappy ending pleases the novelist. He has set out on a voyage and announced, I have failed and must set out again. If you create a happy ending, there is a somewhat false sense of having solved life's problems.'

CHECK THE NET

For a series of ideas about and images of Lyme Regis and the area, visit **www.soton.ac.uk~imw**

CONTEXT

Darwin and other scientists of the nineteenth century put forward ideas about creation and evolution that challenged traditional views of the biblical version of Creation. Charles Lyell (1797–1875), whose geological theories supported Darwinism, also challenged beliefs about time, later referred to as 'deep time', in geology. The threat to religion from Darwinism lies at the basis of the argument between Charles and Ernestina's father.

A couple, Charles Smithson and Ernestina Freeman, walk along the Cobb. They notice a dark figure at the far end of the rampart, staring out to sea. It is March 1867. The author comments on attitudes towards the Cobb through the centuries. There is mention of a 'local spy'.

In Chapter 2 Charles and Ernestina talk of their coming marriage as they walk on the Cobb, and we hear that here is disagreement between Charles and Ernestina's father over the issue of Darwinism.

Charles, concerned for the safety of the woman on the Cobb, speaks to her. She does not speak, but Charles feels pierced by her eyes.

In Chapter 3 Charles reflects on his life. He seems financially secure, having a small inheritance and the expectation of more from his unmarried uncle. His studies at Cambridge were unfinished. He has spent time travelling and has developed an interest in palaeontology. He has avoided any possible engagements to eligible young ladies.

COMMENTARY

Fowles's narrator imitates the Victorian use of epigraphs. The first epigraph, Hardy's 'The Riddle', matches the image of the woman on the Cobb. In imitating the Victorian novel from a modern perspective, the **narrative** has elements of **pastiche** and **parody**.

The narrator quotes guidebooks, and juxtaposes historical **allusions** (the Armada, the seventeenth-century Monmouth rebellion, Michelangelo) with modern references (beach huts, taxes, Henry Moore), thus offering a wide perspective on events.

The question 'I exaggerate?' invites the reader to make his or her own judgement. Direct address in the second person ('if you had turned northward …') intersperses the third-person narrative, while mention of the spy engages interest, but the idea is not fully explored. The emphatic aside ('and there was one') suggests more will be heard of this subject.

The figure at the end of the Cobb is described in timeless terms: 'a figure from myth', 'a living memorial'. Repetition of 'staring, staring' and the word 'motionless' suggest a fixed purpose (p. 11). There is danger in the stare, which is 'like a rifle' and then a 'lance' (pp. 15–16). The setting with high winds and the 'madness of the empty sea' accentuates the danger. The woman is enigmatic. The description of her in negative terms ('there was no artifice there …') suggests that the opposites of these statements may well be relevant. The phrase 'again and again, afterwards' implies that the impression will remain with Charles (p. 16). The encounter, which lasted 'two or three seconds at most', is the first of several pivotal moments in the narrative.

The class difference between Charles and Ernestina is shown. Charles regards this in a frivolous manner: referring to the disagreement with her father over Darwin and man's descent from apes, he reflects that his grandfather was 'a titled ape' (p. 13). The issue of money is raised, as Ernestina is the daughter of a rich merchant, and Charles the potential inheritor of his uncle's wealth. The changing fashions for women at this time are portrayed in the descriptions of the clothes worn by Ernestina. In the mid nineteenth century, new materials, dyes and designs allowed women to show greater freedom of expression in their choice of clothing compared to the dull and constricting fashions of the earlier part of the century.

Charles's dilettante studies in palaeontology are put into perspective by Ernestina's revelation that he has been walking over the stones of the Cobb that contain the very fossils he is supposed to be studying. It is Ernestina who mentions the reference to the Cobb in *Persuasion*, where Louisa Musgrove falls from the stone inserts in the wall (*Persuasion*, Chapter 12). Ernestina's teasing of Charles as 'the scientist, the despiser of novels' introduces two important aspects of theme and character (p. 14).

In Chapter 3 Charles's 'tranquil boredom' is relieved in his study of palaeontology. His past affairs with prostitutes underline Victorian, male-dominated ambivalence to sexual encounters. Charles has rejected writing, politics and science as possible future occupations, though he may be using the high sights he set for himself as excuses,

QUESTION

Look closely at the first encounter between Charles and Sarah Woodruff. What do you note about the language and the images in the narrative?

CHECK THE BOOK

Ellen Pifer notes that 'as an experimental writer testing the conventional assumptions about reality he [Fowles] examines and parodies the traditional devices of storytelling' (*Dictionary of Literary Biography*, Vol. 8).

CHECK THE BOOK

In Chapter 11 of *Persuasion* Jane Austen describes a visit to Lyme, and in Chapter 12 she relates the accidental fall of Louisa Musgrove on the Cobb (Penguin Classics, pp. 116–18 and pp. 128–36).

CONTEXT

The 'German Jew' mentioned on page 18 is Karl Marx (1813–83), co-author with Engels of *The Communist Manifesto* and author of *Das Kapital*, which developed his theories of capitalism and class struggle.

CHECK THE FILM

Reread Chapter 1 and then watch the opening two-minute sequence of the film of *The French Lieutenant's Woman*. Compare the ways in which the film represents what is happening to the narrative structure of the novel.

and his role as an intelligent idler is established. His avoidance of potential marriages reveals cynicism and an unwillingness to commit to relationships.

The revelation that he has not yet found the right girl comes at the end of Chapter 3, yet we have seen that Charles is engaged to be married in Chapter 1. This flashback puts the present relationship with Ernestina in some doubt. It also indicates that in the **narrative** there may be shifts in time as well as overt **anachronistic allusions**.

GLOSSARY

9	**eponym** a name derived from another, in this case the name of the place
	Piraeus chief port of Greece, close to Athens
	Armada the Spanish Armada, a fleet of ships sent to attack England in 1588 but defeated by the English fleet and then almost completely destroyed by storms
	Monmouth the Duke of Monmouth (1649–85), who led a rebellion against King James II to contest the crown; he was captured and executed
10	**Henry Moore … Michelangelo** two sculptors, one from the twentieth century (Henry Moore, 1898–1986), the other from the sixteenth century (Michelangelo, 1475–1564)
	crinoline the hooped, framed petticoat beneath the skirt
	chignon hair knotted or in a roll at the back of the head
11	**dundrearies** long side whiskers, popular in earlier Victorian times
	aniline a product of coal tar, which in the mid nineteenth century was used in dyeing fabrics to produce new colours, such the magenta of the skirt Ernestina is wearing
	mole a sea wall, breakwater or harbour protection, in this case the Cobb
12	**Neptune** the Roman god of the sea
13	*Et voila tout* and that's everything (French)
14	**oolite** a type of limestone, rich in fossils, like the example here referred to by its Latin name
18	*adagio* slowly (musical term)

Chartists members of the short-lived reform movement in England in the nineteenth century (1838–48)

cromlechs … menhirs stones from the Neolithic period, the former a circle of stones, the latter a single stone

19   **Almack's** a London gentleman's club for gambling

baccarat a card game in which players gamble against the banker

Great Bustard a large bird which became extinct in England in the nineteenth century

octoroon having one eighth black ancestry

20   **the Thirty-nine Articles** a set of statements that define the doctrine of the Church of England

Oxford Movement a movement within the Church of England, beginning in 1833; it traced the Church back to early Christian times and attempted to restore High Church ideals

propria terra its own territory (Latin)

voyant trop pour nier … seeing too much to deny and too little to be certain (French)

agnostic one who believes that knowledge of a Supreme Being is impossible; the term was coined by Thomas Huxley in 1869–70

deist … pantheist subscribers to two religious beliefs, the former asserting that the existence of God can be based on natural reason, the latter that God can be identified in the universe or in natural forces

21   *infra dig* unbecoming, from the Latin *infra dignitatum* (beneath one's dignity)

conversazione gatherings for conversation, usually on learned matters (Italian)

22   **Macaulay** Thomas Macaulay (1800–59), popular nineteenth-century historian, famous for his *History of England*

Byronic the Romantic poet Lord Byron (1788–1824) dramatised himself as a gloomy and brooding man of mystery

damp powder damp gunpowder will not fire; therefore, the general sense of action destined to fail

CONTEXT

The two opposing politicians mentioned on page 22 are Benjamin Disraeli (1804–81), Conservative politician and novelist, and William Ewart Gladstone (1809–98), Liberal politician, prime minister from 1868 to 1874 and in 1880, and finally from 1886 to 1894. Later in the narrative their interchangeability is **satirised** in the names 'Mr Gladraeli' and 'Mr Dizzystone' (p. 104).

CHAPTERS 4–6

- Mrs Poulteney's rather grim household and her equally grim beliefs are outlined.
- We learn how Sarah Woodruff was taken in as an assistant by Mrs Poulteney on the advice of the vicar.
- Ernestina's character and appearance are described while she stays at her Aunt Tranter's.
- We learn of Sarah's immediate history and present difficulties, one of which is jealousy of her on the part of Mrs Fairley, the housekeeper.

? QUESTION

Read the epigraphs to Chapter 4. What does the extract from Mrs Norton's poem suggest about love and the afterlife? The footnote on page 35 will develop your response.

Following a portrayal of the gloomy house of the widow Mrs Poulteney, we learn that a year previously the Vicar of Lyme suggested Sarah Woodruff as an assistant for her. In charge of the servants in the household is the unpleasant, sadistic Mrs Fairley.

In Chapter 5 Ernestina Freeman, in her room furnished in ornate style, contemplates her sexuality but is daunted by all aspects of it.

In Chapter 6 the vicar provides some detail about Sarah's life as the daughter of a tenant farmer and about her present state. She had been educated and had served as governess. The head of the family in which she worked had taken in a lieutenant from a French ship that had been driven ashore in a storm. Sarah, who had been taught French, supervised his convalescence. A relationship developed. Sarah followed the lieutenant to Weymouth in the belief that he would marry her. She was condemned for her actions.

Sarah was brought to Mrs Poulteney's and interviewed. Mrs Poulteney agreed to accept her in the belief that she was offering salvation to Sarah, but really she wished to assure her own salvation. The prime motive was to gain advantage over Lady Cotton, a woman in the neighbourhood noted for her charitable involvements, though with a similar self-seeking and severe piety. Sarah agreed to enter the household because of the view over the sea and the simple fact she had 'exactly seven pence in the world' (p. 42).

COMMENTARY

The portraits of Mrs Poulteney and Mrs Fairley are Dickensian in spirit. The women are well suited to share a household, each displaying unpleasant characteristics. The **satire** of their nastiness and moral righteousness is presented with relish. The catalogue of ex-employees is amusingly lengthy, and the 'disgraceful and cowardly nature' of their leaving **ironically** queried by the narrator (p. 25). Cruelty is portrayed in the likening of Mrs Poulteney to a 'plump vulture', the reference to her fondness for the 'forest of humane man-traps' that protect her house and the **anachronistic allusion** to a place for her in the Gestapo (p. 26). Her relationships with the servants show cruelty in the guise of respectability. Her religious beliefs are superficial: fear of damnation colours her motives. The vicar's revenge on her condescension and her desire to perform good deeds in order to gain salvation is described amusingly as 'not absolutely unconnected with malice' (p. 30). The outcome of his less than charitable thought is, ironically, an act of charity. Mrs Poulteney will take in a distressing case, a part of whose story is revealed by the vicar. And it is just a part, for it is stated in an ironic aside that the vicar omitted some detail.

Sarah's story is revealed in instalments from various sources. In Chapter 1 we had gossip and rumour. Here we have a story, with careful omissions, told by the vicar (pp. 36–40). Later in Chapter 6 we have more detail and more omissions from Mr Fursey-Harris, the vicar of nearby Charmouth (p. 40). This structural device, from start to finish, surrounds Sarah with an air of the unknowable.

The portrayal of Ernestina in Chapter 5 is as a prim young lady of her times. The only child of a wealthy tradesman, she has led a sheltered life. Her room is furnished in an ornate style, in contrast to the heavy Victorian style of the rest of the house. She is at first sight a rich, slightly pampered Victorian girl. However, the comparison to Becky Sharp, the scheming protagonist in Thackeray's *Vanity Fair* (1847–8), introduces a cunning aspect that also appears elsewhere. Ernestina is conscious of class difference. The old order of society, represented by Charles and his uncle, was giving way at this time to a new order of self-made men like

CHECK THE BOOK

William Palmer also draws comparison with Dickens: 'Another starkly realised Dickensian character in *The French Lieutenant's Woman* is the grotesque Mrs Poulteney, who mimics the style and attitudes of characters like the evil dwarf Quilp in *The Old Curiosity Shop* or Madame Lafarge in *A Tale of Two Cities* or Miss Wade in *Little Dorrit*, characters whose lives are so warped that their only pleasure comes from the persecution of other human beings' (*The Fiction of John Fowles: Tradition, Art and the Loneliness of Selfhood*, 1974, pp. 24–5).

CHECK THE NET

For an understanding of how the stratification of mid-Victorian classes was evolving into a new order populated by new 'creatures' such as Mr Freeman and Sam Farrer, visit **www.bbc.co.uk** and type 'History Victorian' into the search box.

CONTEXT

Fowles has his narrator place Ernestina in both historical and fictional contexts. Fowles is taking a **postmodernist** position of seeing reality as a construct, just as his fiction is. There will be other instances in the novel where the reader is invited to engage with the creator of the fiction in what Samuel Taylor Coleridge termed 'the willing suspension of disbelief' (*Biographia Literaria*, 1817).

Ernestina's father, who saw marriage as a movement into the upper classes. Changes were also taking place in the ambitions of the working classes, epitomised in Charles's servant, Sam.

Marriage will give Ernestina the freedom from parental control that she desires, but it also brings fear of sexual intimacy. Her ambivalent attitude to her sexuality (pp. 34–5) is shown in the pleasure she takes in admiring herself in the mirror being immediately followed by references that present sex, for the typically Victorian girl, as something cruel (wolves howling), painful (the Laocoön statue) and animalistic (the violence of animals coupling).

Ernestina displays shallowness in her jealousy of Mary and her petulant treatment of Charles, who is 'forbidden ever to look again at any woman under the age of sixty' (p. 32). However, we are reminded that Ernestina is resilient, as the twentieth-century **narrative** perspective informs us that she will survive well into the twentieth century, dying 'on the day that Hitler invaded Poland' (p. 33). This **anachronistic** detail teases the reader into considering Ernestina from the 'now' of 1867 to her end in 1939.

GLOSSARY

24	**arsenic** a poisonous substance released from, in this case, the green paint on the walls
25	**Stygian** adjective coming from Styx, the river in Hades
26	**Gestapo** the Nazi secret police, renowned for brutality
27	**Low Church** within the Church of England, those placing emphasis on belief in the Gospels rather than on rituals
	one-tenth a tithe, or tenth part of one's personal income, given to support the Church
28	**the Rock** symbolic idea of the Church or Heaven
	de haut en bas … de bas en haut from high to low … from low to high (French)
31	**Phiz** pseudonym of H. K. Browne, a Victorian artist noted for his illustrations of Dickens's works
	John Leech Victorian illustrator and caricaturist (1817–64)
32	**Prinny** nickname of the Prince Regent, the future King George IV

33	*bouderies* sulking or pouting
34	apostrophize turning away from ordinary speech to address oneself as another person
	peignoir a light dressing gown
	Laocoön in Greek mythology, Laocoön and his sons were killed by sea serpents
35	Satyr-shaped in the shape of the half-man, half-animal god of nature in Greek and Roman mythologies
	Freud Sigmund Freud (1856–1939), the founder of psychoanalysis (see **Contemporary approaches: Psychological approaches**)
	Id the mass of primitive instincts in the subconscious mind
36	Treitschke German historian (1834–96)
	camphor an oil with a bitter-sweet odour, used as a moth repellent to protect fabrics
39	Patmos a Greek island in the Aegean Sea
41	*Dies Irae* a hymn used in the mass for the dead; from the Latin, meaning the Day of Wrath and applied to the Day of Judgement
	egregious adjective with shades of meaning from prominent to outrageous
	McLuhan Marshall McLuhan (1911–80), Canadian writer on mass media, popular in the 1960s

CHAPTERS 7–8

- The relationship between Charles and his man-servant Sam, and the latter's interest in Mary, are explored.
- Nineteenth-century interest in natural science is described.
- Charles searches for fossils on Ware Commons.

Charles wakes to a pleasant morning, confident in the order of his world. He talks with Sam, who has met Mary, Aunt Tranter's maid. Mary has made fun of Sam, and he is disgruntled about this.

 CHECK THE NET

For an informative and pictorially excellent website showing the geology around Lyme Regis and palaeontological finds from the area visit **www. discoveringfossils. co.uk/lyme_regis_ fossils.htm**

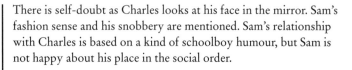

CONTEXT

For a brief note on the language of the nineteenth-century Cockney, the language of Sam Farrer, see *London in the Nineteenth Century* by Jerry White, 2008, pp. 111–13.

There is self-doubt as Charles looks at his face in the mirror. Sam's fashion sense and his snobbery are mentioned. Sam's relationship with Charles is based on a kind of schoolboy humour, but Sam is not happy about his place in the social order.

Chapter 8 sees Charles with a free day when Ernestina says that she feels ill. Detail of the geology of the Lyme coast, an area rich in fossils, is given. A little overdressed, Charles sets out along the coast. He notices that time has passed and the tide is coming in, though he is in no danger. He sees a path leading up from the beach into woodland.

COMMENTARY

Pleasant images ('the warm air', 'a rider clopped peacefully down to the sea') permeate the first three paragraphs (pp. 43–4). Mention of Proust, the author of *A la recherche du temps perdu* (*In Search of Lost Time* or *Remembrance of Things Past*) draws attention to the use of images that evoke impressions of memory.

QUESTION

Sam Weller appears in *The Pickwick Papers* (1836–7), by Charles Dickens. What is achieved by this **allusion** to a servant from thirty years before the time of Sam Farrer? Think in terms of time and change and also in terms of the narrative perspective. (For an idea of the portrayal of Sam Weller, see Chapter 16 of Dickens's novel.)

Charles's confidence in and certainty of the order of things ('so much assurance of position, order, calm, civilization', p. 43) colour the interlude with Sam. The relationship between the privileged master and the servant thwarted in his ambitions is based on banter and light-hearted but firm control. Glimpses of an edge in the relationship can be detected and they feature increasingly as the **narrative** unfolds. However, Sam's dissatisfaction is put into a broader socio-historical context. Sam represents the emerging working classes, unsettled and dissatisfied with their lot and prepared to do something about it. He is placed in his present context by historical references: back thirty years to 'the immortal Weller' of Charles Dickens, and then forward one hundred years to the 'mod of the 1960s'. The reader is asked to consider time in more than just the chronological sense. Charles's failure to recognise the 'social revolution' is the first of his many failures to see things clearly.

The image of Charles in the mirror (pp. 45–6) permits self-examination, but the word 'mask' places 'the ambiguous face' in a different light. What Charles sees is duly recorded, but the acknowledgement of 'a faintly foolish face' is not given serious attention in the midst of general self-approval, which is apparent in his wink at himself in the mirror. The **irony** of his thoughts – 'Breeding and self-knowledge, he most legibly had' (p. 46) – shows that he sees his reflection but does not penetrate his own mask.

In Chapter 8 we see Ernestina's pampered existence. Her taking to her bed conveniently allows Charles freedom to go on his expedition to Ware Commons to search for tests – echinoderms found in the rock strata. 'Expedition' is indeed the correct word in the light of the humorously drawn description of Charles and his equipment (p. 51). Our amusement, however, is put into perspective by the narrator, who reminds us that amateurs such as Charles were the ones who would lay 'the foundations of all our modern science' (p. 52).

The **satirical** portrait of the Victorian amateur scientist is softened by the human moment when he removes his boots, gaiters and stockings in order to paddle. The satire is also softened by the juxtaposition of the fact that Charles had not yet fully understood Darwin with the fact that neither had Darwin himself.

The Darwinian idea of the 'survival of the fittest' reassures Charles of his position in the evolutionary scheme of things. The collapse of the Linnaean ladder, the *Scala Naturae*, however, does not enter Charles's head, even when he holds an example of such a collapse in his hands. Nor does the thought of emergent new species bother him, though the observant reader will have detected that new social beings were also evolving.

 QUESTION

Charles looks at his reflection in the mirror. What does he see, but equally importantly, what does he not see? Compare this with other incidents in the narrative that involve reflections in mirrors.

 CHECK THE BOOK

A description of Ware Commons is found in H. Rowland Brown's *The Beauties of Lyme Regis*, written in 1857: 'Before us, we see a number of hills, which after a succession of Land-slips, are broken in various directions, into almost every imaginable shape; these enshrine numberless little dells, carpeted by the softest turf, covered with luxuriant copse-wood, and festooned with the blossoms of the wild rose, white clematis, and wild convolvulus.'

GLOSSARY

44	*quod est demonstrandum* which is to demonstrate (Latin), often abbreviated to 'q.e.d.'
	ergo therefore (Latin)
46	Doric in the style of ancient Greece
	coruscated sparkling with reflected flashes of light
	Beau Brummell an English dandy and fashion-conscious gentleman, a one-time friend of Prinny, the Prince Regent (later George IV)

continued

CONTEXT

Mary Anning (p. 50) was an English palaeontologist (1799–1847), who discovered the fossil skeleton of an ichthyosaurus, which is now in the British Museum. She sold rocks and fossils from her shop in Lyme Regis (it is suggested that the tongue twister *She sells sea shells by the sea shore* referred to her).

47   'mod' member of a 1960s teenage group with a distinctive neat style of dress

Sancho Panza the squire/servant of Don Quixote in the novel of the same name, by the Spanish writer Miguel de Cervantes (1547–1616)

Dorothea an early Christian saint, usually represented with images of roses and fruit

Leslie Stephen English scholar, critic and author (1829–94)

50   *Ichthyosaurus platyodon* an extinct sea creature with a fish-like body and a long snout

anningii of Anning (Latin), a part-classification of a species using the discoverer's name

Isocrina a term no longer in common use but presumably a group of fossils of sea creatures such as echinoderms or crinoids

tests from Latin *testa*, a hard shell

51   Baedeker Karl Baedeker (1801–59), publisher of definitive guide books that still carry his name today

53   Homer ancient Greek poet

The Voyage of the Beagle Darwin served as naturalist on HMS *Beagle*, undertaking a scientific survey of the seas off South America; he published several accounts of the voyage and his discoveries

oubliette a cell or dungeon, with no opening other than in the roof, where a prisoner could be left and forgotten (from the French *oublier*, to forget)

Linnaean adjective relating to Linnaeus (1707–78), the Swedish naturalist famous for the double-naming classification of animals and plants

Scala Naturae the ladder of nature (Latin), sometimes called the Great Chain of Being: the belief in the order of life from rocks and minerals at the bottom rising through plants, primitive animals, the higher animals, man, spiritual beings and finally to God

nulla species nova no new species (Latin)

54   *exempli gratia* for example (Latin), shortened to 'e.g.'

lias a type of limestone, rich in fossils

ammonite a shell fossil coiled in the shape of a ram's horn

CHAPTERS 9–10

- Sarah's influence in the Poulteney household is shown.
- Mrs Fairley acts as a willing spy on Sarah during her walks. She sees Sarah on Ware Commons.
- There is a detailed description of the Undercliff, its beauties and its dangers.
- Charles comes across Sarah in the Undercliff, the eastern section of Ware Commons.

Sarah has been with Mrs Poulteney for over a year. We learn how, after her error in following the French lieutenant, Sarah was deserted. She was dismissed from her post as governess to Mrs Talbot's children and faced destitution. Sarah was and still is regarded as an outcast. She possesses an uncanny insight into the character of people, and this quality has caused her to reject several potential suitors, who seemed insincere.

Sarah's influence in the house creates a pleasant atmosphere among the servants. Her voice when she reads from the Bible has a profound effect. Her walking out alone disturbs Mrs Poulteney. Mrs Fairley, the housekeeper, relishes spying on her. Sarah is questioned about the way she constantly looks out to sea, and is requested to walk elsewhere. She complies, which is how she comes to visit Ware Commons. That she does so is reported by Mrs Fairley to Mrs Poulteney, who reacts with shock.

In Chapter 10 Ware Commons is described. Charles takes the path into the Undercliff. As he searches for fossils, he comes across a woman asleep on a ledge in the rocks. It is Sarah, and he observes her closely. She wakes, and he apologises for his intrusion. He continues up the path.

COMMENTARY

The fact that Mrs Talbot 'knew Sarah faced penury' is **ironically** qualified by images from sensationalist Victorian fiction (p. 56). The

CHECK THE BOOK

Commenting on Sarah's education, Barry N. Olshen suggests, 'She has been given the trappings of a lady without the social standing; she has been forced out of her own class without being raised to the next. If there is a key to her actions, it lies in the combination of these seemingly determining circumstances and what she does to break the mold they have cast for her' (*John Fowles*, p. 74).

QUESTION

What qualities do you detect in Mrs Fairley that make her a suitably unpleasant housekeeper for Mrs Poulteney? Look at what she says and does and at her interaction with other characters.

'starving heroine', the 'snow-covered doorsteps', the suicidal plunge with 'lightning', the 'cruel heads of pursuers', and the cloak like 'a falling raven's wing of terrible death' **parody** illustrations in the 'edifying tales' of Mrs Sherwood.

Sarah's education raises her above her class, but she is unable to participate fully in the class she enters. She represents the Victorian governess who has the 'veneer of a lady' but is a 'victim of a caste society'(p. 58).

Sarah's humane treatment of the servants contrasts with the cruelty of Mrs Poulteney. Sarah deals competently with her mistress, leading her into 'the perverse pleasures of seeming truly kind' in dealing with Mary (p. 60). Comment is expressed in the modern idiom ('Sarah had twigged Mrs Poulteney') and the broader historical perspective of the image of 'a skilled cardinal' handling 'a weak pope'.

Sarah's liberty comes on the advice of Dr Grogan, though we may later wonder whether Sarah had manipulated this situation.

Chapter 9 ends with the shock revelation that Sarah is frequenting Ware Commons, a place of ill repute, and Chapter 10 begins as Charles makes his way to this same wild area. The early paragraphs provide a description of the Undercliff, which is the eastern section of Ware Commons, but for dramatic effect this information is not revealed until the end of the section. The area provides a luxuriant 'dark cascade of trees', and 'green Brazilian chasms'. There is a sense of the 'joyous indiscipline' of nature, as well as danger in the 'deep chasms' and 'desolation'. Before the 'English Garden of Eden' is mentioned (p. 71), the reader will have picked up essential elements of this **allusion** as Charles and Sarah move closer together.

In a time shift, we are invited to view the area as if in aerial flight above it (p. 70). The isolation is seen both as in the past and as in the present: it is 'slightly less solitary a hundred years ago than it is today'. Charles's inability to savour the pleasure of the moment is put into historical perspective (p. 72). Reference to the Renaissance brings forth the maxim 'What is, is good'. However, the Victorian

CHECK THE BOOK
Sarah's position is similar to that of Tess in Thomas Hardy's *Tess of the d'Urbervilles* (1891). Kevin Padian points out 'the stamp of ancestry' and 'the contradiction between her family's ancient status and its present one, and her family's pretensions to nobility that eventually ruin her'. He concludes, 'Tess shares with Sarah Woodruff this slide in status, the result of vain aspirations of parents who make their daughters fit for neither world' ('Deep Time, Evolutionary Legacy and Darwinian Landscape', in James Aubrey, ed., *John Fowles* and *Nature*, 1999).

age's inability to grasp this idea is expressed in the contrast between the possibility of 'I possess this now, therefore I am happy' and the reality of 'I cannot possess this for ever, and therefore am sad'. Charles believes he is 'too pampered, too spoilt by civilisation ever to inhabit nature again'.

As Charles realises the time, his '*duty* towards Ernestina' contrasts with his '*lust* for echinoderms'. The upward path Charles takes 'forked without indication': the lower path, 'already deeply shadowed', and the upper path, 'where he could plainly orientate himself', suggest more than a mere choice of way. There is **irony** in that the upper path does not orientate Charles. It is here on the edge of the cliffs that he stumbles upon 'a figure' that at first he thinks is 'a corpse' (pp. 73–5). (Analysis of this incident is to be found in the **Extended commentaries**.)

GLOSSARY

58	**Walter Scott** Scottish novelist and poet (1771–1832)
	caste a particular social class
62	*Eli, Eli, lama sabachthani* an Aramaic phrase from Matthew's gospel, the words of Christ on the cross: 'My God, my God, why have you abandoned me?'
	antimacassar a cloth covering for the backs of chairs to protect the fabric from macassar hair oil
65	**barouche** a four-wheeled carriage with a retractable hood
66	**Blue Vinny** a type of veined cheese from Dorset
	Black Ven an area of the coast near Lyme Regis with landslips and terraced cliffs
67	**Satan's sails** Mrs Poulteney's term for the sails of the French lieutenant's ship
68	**stays** corsets with bones to shape the figure.
71	**arbutus ... ilex ... clematis** wild flowering plants
72	**Chesil Bank** an eight-mile stretch of shingle beach from Portland to Abbotsbury
	Gibraltar the limestone rocky southernmost point of Spain
	Portland Bill the limestone southernmost tip of Chesil Bank

continued

CONTEXT

'The Undercliff is one of the most geologically dynamic areas of England, prone to rockfalls, landslides and "subsidence", the inward collapse of many acres of land. "The land courts the sea here," Fowles's old neighbour growled when they met. "T'is sidling land"' (Eileen Warburton, quoting John Fowles's diaries, in *John Fowles: A Life in Two Worlds*, 2004, pp. 279–80).

CONTEXT

The German dramatist Bertolt Brecht (1898–1956) coined the term *verfremdungs-seffekt*, an alienating technique distancing the audience from the illusory world of the theatre (referred to on p. 62).

CONTEXT

Jean-Jacques Rousseau (1712–78) was a French philosopher, educationist and writer. The idea of the noble savage, referred to on page 72, was central to Rousseau's belief that primitive man was happy in natural surroundings before being corrupted by modern civilisation.

72	Renaissance a period in European history (fourteenth to sixteenth century) that saw a revival of classical art forms
	Botticelli Sandro Botticelli (1444–1510), an Italian artist who used naturalistic detail in his paintings
	Ronsard Pierre de Ronsard (1524–85), a French poet whose works were revived by the Romantics of the nineteenth century
73	hegemony leadership
	echinoderms primitive marine creatures, such as starfish and sea urchins
	scuts the short, erect tails of rabbits
	eyebright … birdsfoot … marjoram more examples of the rich plantlife in the Undercliff
	wideawake a type of hat with a very wide brim

CHAPTERS 11–12

QUESTION

Fowles often compares and contrasts pairs of characters, here clearly inviting the reader to consider Mrs Tranter and her relationship with Mary, and then to look at the relationship between Mrs Poulteney and Sarah. What effects are created here in terms of character, sympathies and social comment?

- Ernestina spends the morning at home, while Charles walks on Ware Commons.
- Ernestina's family background is given.
- Charles sees Sarah emerge from the wood and attempts further apology.
- Sarah remains distant and returns to Lyme alone.
- The narrator observes Sarah, in a distraught state, at her window.

In a flashback to the beginning of the day, we see Charles go out to look for fossils, while Ernestina, apparently ill, remains in her room. Ernestina is jealous of Mary, whom she believes to be flirting with Charles. Mary is popular with Mrs Tranter, who enjoys her companionship when they are alone in the house. Ernestina warns Mary about her meetings with Sam. She turns to her diary to pass the time.

Chapter 11 gives us Ernestina's background. Her grandfather, a draper, had expanded his business into a larger department store. We learn how Ernestina contrived to meet Charles, an eligible suitor. Charles suddenly decided that he should marry. When he proposed, Ernestina started to cry. Mr Freeman was pleased with the match, while Charles was somewhat bewildered.

In Chapter 12 we return to Ware Commons, where Charles ascends the path. The farmer at the Dairy, noticing Sarah emerge from the woods, calls her 'the French Loot'n'nts Hoer' (p. 88). Charles sees Sarah on the path to Lyme. He catches up with her, again apologises, and offers to accompany her. She insists on returning alone.

Charles calls at Mrs Tranter's. He tells Ernestina of his day, but omits to mention the meeting with Sarah. The history of Ware Commons is given, and its reputation as a meeting place for lovers.

Mrs Poulteney berates Sarah for frequenting Ware Commons. Sarah's protests are quelled by Mrs Poulteney's indignation. Sarah agrees to avoid the place. The chapter ends as the narrator stands that night below Sarah's window. He considers the possibility of her jumping from the window. However, he knows that she is alive a fortnight after this incident. The final words of the chapter are enigmatic: 'Who is Sarah? Out of what shadows does she come?' (p. 96).

COMMENTARY

The language describing Ernestina starts with 'sulkily', moves through 'displeasure' and 'vexed' to 'frowned sourly and reproachfully' (pp. 76–7). Her thoughts about Mary and her fears about Charles's past add to an unsympathetic portrayal at this point. The Victorian diktat regarding 'sinful speculation' on all matters verging on the physical or sexual, however, should be seen in terms of the wider constraints of the Victorian age.

Reference to Mary's great-great-granddaughter highlights the years that both separate and connect events and people. We are aware of little time disjoints: the sprig of jasmine in Ernestina's diary (p. 81)

CHECK THE BOOK

Thomas C. Foster places Ernestina in a historical perspective: 'Ernestina, with her love of bright colours, her adherence to the latest fashions, and her rejection of some of the more outmoded Victorian strictures, stands as a thoroughly "modern" young woman, vintage 1867. Yet her modernity is very much of her time; that is to say, she is as up-to-date as a girl could manage while remaining firmly in her own era' (*Understanding John Fowles*, pp. 76–7).

was a playful love token in the conservatory (p. 85), since which time things have changed.

The qualities uniting Ernestina and Charles ('a superiority of intelligence, a lightness of touch, a dryness') suggest little emotion. The 'spoilt daughter' with her 'wildly determined' nature makes Charles 'the real prey', caught by the planting of the 'fatal seed' – the adjective conveying more than just Charles's immediate fate. The courtship is doubly **ironic** (pp. 82–6), for Ernestina is literally and metaphorically led 'down the aisle of hothouse plants' while Charles is seen **anachronistically** as a spaceman, 'not quite sure which planet he had landed on'.

From the artificial hothouse, the scene moves to natural woods where Charles, about to follow a path, sees 'a black figure' emerging from the trees. Two of Sarah's enigmatic qualities emerge: her look, which 'seemed both to envelop him and reject him', and her elusiveness, 'a figure in a dream, both standing still and yet always receding' (p. 89). Charles realises that the 'innocent woods' enable her to escape from her condemnation. His decision not to tell of these meetings is ironic, when Ernestina playfully asks if he has been 'dallying with the wood-nymphs'. Charles feels that it would be a lie 'to dismiss those two encounters lightly', but then there is the idea that 'silence seemed finally less a falsehood in that trivial room' (p. 91).

The hyperbole in the 'Sodom and Gomorrah' image in Mrs Poulteney's mind takes us back a fortnight in time. The 'Bosch-like picture of Ware Commons' (pp. 91–3) and her vivid imaginings are possibly induced by laudanum, humorously compared to sedative pill addiction in the twentieth-century novel by Jacqueline Susann, *The Valley of the Dolls* (1966). Mrs Poulteney is compared to 'some pagan idol' with 'a stone face', demanding a 'blood-sacrifice' (p. 95).

CHECK THE BOOK

Patricia Waugh suggests a way of looking at Fowles's 'frame-breaks', where the narrator enters into his fiction, as at the end of Chapter 12: 'The alternation of frame and frame-break (or the construction of an illusion through the imperceptibility of the frame) provides the essential deconstructive method of metafiction' (*Metafiction: The Theory and Practice of Self-Conscious Fiction*, 1988, p. 31).

GLOSSARY

76	jonquils a species of the narcissus flower
77	*grisette* a French working girl
	Cintra also Sintra, a town near Lisbon in Portugal
	Occam's ... razor a principle for use in analysis; it states that the simplest explanation is the best choice
	Waterloo 1815 battle in Belgium at which Napoleon was defeated, ending the Napoleonic Wars
	Flora the Roman goddess of flowers
	rondelet rounded or plump (French)
79	*soubrettes* lively young female servants (French)
80	*à la mode* fashionable (French)
	brimless topper a fashionable hat without a brim
	saffron an orange powder derived from the crocus
	Don Juan Spanish nobleman noted for his sexual exploits
81	plutocratic stratification the ordering of the classes according to wealth
83	Early Cretaceous in geology, a period in the Mesozoic era
84	Haymarket central London area of theatres and, in the nineteenth century, the haunt of prostitutes
85	stephanotis a waxy, scented flower
88	Jeremiah in the Bible, the prophet who foresaw doom and grief
	penny ... charming heads pre-decimalisation coin bearing the head of the young Queen Victoria, still in circulation in the mid twentieth century
	Hoer crude **dialect** form for 'whore'
90	*Noli me tangere* do not touch me (Latin), words spoken by Jesus to Mary Magdalene, in the garden after the resurrection
	déshabille dressed in a disorderly manner (French)
	navigator a builder of a navigation or canal, shortened to 'navvy'
91	ammonitiferous bearing ammonite shells
	Hercules legendary Roman who performed twelve labours that demanded superhuman strength
	wood-nymphs in mythology, spirits of nature depicted as beautiful maidens

continued

QUESTION

Why do you think Charles's significant meetings with Sarah take place on Ware Commons? Consider the place's history, its nature, society, **symbolism** and plot development.

CONTEXT

Opium and laudanum, an alcoholic solution of the same drug, mentioned on page 94, were regularly used in the nineteenth century. Samuel Taylor Coleridge (1772–1834) took opium, under the influence of which he is said to have written the poem 'Kubla Khan'.

91	Sodom and Gomorrah ancient sinful cities in the Bible, destroyed by God
92	enclosure acts Acts of Parliament between 1709 and 1869 whereby private land had to be fenced off
	Anschluss unification (German); a political annexing of one country by another
	de facto as a matter of fact (Latin)
93	draconian extremely severe, derived from Draco, a Greek lawmaker who demanded the death penalty for most offences
	myxomatosis a disease introduced into Australia and France in the 1950s to kill rabbits, and which spread to Britain
	Donkey's Green Ball Donkey Green is a grassy area of the Undercliff, where picnics and games took place
	Song of Solomon a short book of the Bible that tells of the courtship of a man and woman
	Godfrey's Cordial one of several patent medicines containing opium, alcohol and various blends of ingredients
	Bosch Hieronymus Bosch (c. 1460–1516), Dutch painter famous for *The Garden of Earthly Delights*
	objective correlative a literary term referring to an explicit representation of an abstract concept or idea
95	paths of righteousness the words are taken from Psalm 23 in the Bible

? QUESTION

In this chapter we are addressed directly by Fowles's narrator. What effects are created by this deliberate intrusion into the **narrative** and direct address to you, the reader?

CHAPTER 13

- Once again the narrator enters into his own narrative directly.
- Fowles poses questions about authorship and narrative in Victorian times and in the present time of writing the novel.
- We return to Sarah, who continues to visit Ware Commons.

The narrator addresses the reader directly. He discusses the problem of a story in which the characters act independently rather than being directed by their creator. The narrator had intended Charles to return to Lyme, but Charles went to the Dairy to ask about Sarah. The narrator acknowledges that the traditional novel is out of fashion according to modern views. He suggests that freedom from a God-like control by the author is required. However, he does acknowledge the artifice of the narrator.

He engages the reader in what is essentially a 'Chinese-box' effect, in which there is first the traditional world of the Victorian characters themselves, then a further dimension in the role of the narrator who at times enters that world and at other times comments on it, and finally, outside of his creation, Fowles the creator of the narrative structure that will provide more than the traditional novel's illusions of reality.

As a reporter of the outward facts, the narrator returns to the recent encounter on Ware Commons. Sarah has continued to visit Ware Commons and has so far avoided being seen.

COMMENTARY

This chapter challenges the reader in its direct address. The narrator simultaneously asserts his authority over the text and admits that he cannot control characters who have an independent autonomy. The Victorian novel's omniscient God-like author is now replaced by a different god, who allows his creatures freedom: 'There is only one good definition of God: the freedom that allows other freedoms to exist' (p. 99). In an existentialist manner, the narrator demonstrates that the old omniscient **narrative** point of view is now interwoven into a modern technique. He thus shows the inadequacy of both the Victorian tradition and the modern *nouveau roman* school of Roland Barthes and Alain Robbe-Grillet.

Reference is made to Thackeray's concluding words in *Vanity Fair*, where the God-like author says, 'Let us shut up the box and the puppets, for our play is played out' (Penguin Classics, p. 809). The modern novelist must avoid this position, if he is to follow the dictates of the *nouveau roman*, which has been defined as the anti-novel. The narrator clearly rejects this theory, and his own assertion, 'Fiction is woven into all', suggests that the lines between the real and the imaginary are impossible to define. 'Fiction' here refers not

CHECK THE BOOK

In **metafiction** the boundaries between illusion and reality are dissolved. There are parallels in drama. Pirandello, in *Six Characters in Search of an Author* (1921), destroys the illusion of the theatre as six 'characters' interrupt rehearsals for a play and demand that their story be told.

CONTEXT

The term *nouveau roman* was first used in 1957 by Émile Henriot to describe the attempts of novelists to create a new style which de-emphasised the traditional aspects of the novel – plot, **narrative**, character, ideas. Alain Robbe-Grillet developed this theory in *Pour un Nouveau Roman*.

only to the author and his novel, the narrator and the story, the characters and their view of things, but even to real life and our own thoughts. Thus, having said that he will conform to the definition of 'freedom that allows other freedoms to exist', the narrator playfully returns to the **narrative** style of the Victorians. In doing this he is poking fun at the modern novel, with its dislike of authorial intervention. He then goes on to demonstrate authorial intrusion in as many subversive ways as possible: **allusions**, footnotes, editorial comment, quotations from the Victorian age, modern references and direct address from the novelist to the reader.

The narrator ensures that the reader is implicated in what he is doing by putting words into our mouths in the colloquial 'Oh, but you say, come on'. He poses almost rhetorical questions: 'I have disgracefully broken the illusion?' and 'But is this preposterous?'. He then makes the **allusion** to Baudelaire's 'hypocrite lecteur', the hypocritical reader addressed in the preface to *Les Fleurs du Mal*, who becomes for the artist 'mon semblable, mon frère' ('my counterpart, my brother'). The reader is seen as similar to the author and as intimate as a brother in the illusion of art, in the 'flight from reality' (p. 99). The narrator draws the reader into the inescapable themes of his artistic creation (Time, Progress, Society, Evolution) and then, in a paraphrase of Baudelaire, he teasingly says, if we refuse to acknowledge them, 'I shall suspect you.'

The narrator, having played with the idea of **metafiction**, now simply claims that he is but a reporter of 'the outward facts'(p. 99). This, too, is quickly seen as another literary game, for he builds up the extended metaphor of the biblical fall and then omnisciently enters into the consciousness of Sarah.

> **CONTEXT**
>
> Charles Baudelaire's preface to *Les Fleurs du Mal* has been quoted often in the context of the reader's close relationship with the author. It is used as a preface to T. S. Eliot's *The Waste Land* and, more recently, Angela Carter used the allusion in *Wise Children* (1992, p. 118).

GLOSSARY	
99	aleatory depending on contingencies or chance
	avant-garde creating or supporting the newest ideas in a particular field
	hypocrite lecteur hypocritical reader (French)

CHAPTERS 14–16

- Charles, Ernestina and Aunt Tranter visit Mrs Poulteney.
- Charles and Ernestina disagree over the relationship between Sam and Mary.
- Charles and Ernestina make up their differences
- Charles agrees to support Sam's courtship of Mary.
- The author makes further intrusions into the story.
- On Ware Commons Charles meets Sarah, who reveals more of her relationship with the French lieutenant.

When Charles, Ernestina and Mrs Tranter visit Mrs Poulteney, Sarah moves as if to leave the room. Mrs Poulteney tells her to stay. During the conversation, Charles notices that Sarah's meekness hides her dislike of Mrs Poulteney. They turn to the subject of Mary, who has been seen talking to Sam. Ernestina states that her behaviour is unacceptable, but Charles and Mrs Tranter take a liberal view. A glance is shared between Charles and Sarah.

In Chapter 15 Charles and Ernestina make up their differences. Ernestina decides to give her green riding dress to Mary. Mary, trying on the dress, admires herself in the mirror. Charles teases Sam about Mary and about his past affairs. He agrees to speak to Mrs Tranter on Sam's behalf.

In Chapter 16, the narrator comments on the tedium of Victorian evenings. On one such evening Ernestina reads a sentimental poem, *The Lady of La Garaye*, during which Charles falls asleep. She throws the book at him. Charles becomes bored with endless talk about the furnishings of their future home. He is allowed to escape the following day.

On Ware Commons he again meets Sarah. He offers her help to get away from Lyme. She states that she has ties to the place. However, she reveals that the French lieutenant will never return, and that he is, in fact, married.

CONTEXT

The chapter endings in *The French Lieutenant's Woman* recreate the episodic quality that characterises much Victorian fiction, notably Dickens's novels. Many Victorian novels were initially published in serial form, only later to appear as books. Each instalment had a 'cliff-hanger' ending that invited audience speculation in the same way that episodes of television soaps do today. Look at the ending of Chapter 14 as an example of this.

 CHECK THE POEM

The Lady of La Garaye is a sentimental, mournful poem, written in 1862 by Mrs Caroline Norton (1808–77), an Irish poet. The extracts on pages 115–16 give you a feel for the style and subject.

CHECK THE BOOK

The portrayal of Mrs Poulteney is given an added dimension in the light of Thomas C. Foster's comments: 'The history of the twentieth century has been one of constant assaults on individuals by a host of totalitarian schemes, among which Hitler is the representative figure. Fowles makes this point clear in his repeated analogies and references in the book to Nazis and those who fought against them' (*Understanding John Fowles*, pp. 76–7).

CHECK THE POEM

For a comparison with the situation between Charles, Ernestina and Sarah in the sitting room at Mrs Poulteney's, read Thomas Hardy's poem 'At Tea' in *Satires of Circumstance* (1914).

COMMENTARY

The social call enables Charles to observe the prejudices of Victorian society. The image of Charles, the 'plump mouse, dropping between the claws of a hungry cat' (p. 102), suggests the anguish of the ordeal.

The narrator's distaste for Mrs Poulteney emerges in the details of her appearance, her tone and her attitude during this 'purgatory' of supposedly polite conversation. The **ironic** distance between Charles's thoughts and his pleasantries of conversation complements this distaste and also provides dark amusement for the reader.

Charles observes Sarah's 'complete disassociation from and disapprobation of her mistress'. His reading of her 'sense of injustice' develops into understanding, which is conveyed in a momentary glance. Recognition of the 'common enemy' is not so much turned personally against Mrs Poulteney as against the bigotry of a judgemental society. The eye contact between Charles and Sarah is different here: her look is no longer the 'lance' that pierced him earlier (p. 16), but 'a look now not through him, but at him' (p. 106).

Ernestina shares in the social prejudice, and contrasts with the understanding between Charles and Sarah. Charles's resolve to teach Ernestina 'an evidently much needed lesson in common humanity' adds to the tension.

In Chapter 15 the reconciliation between Charles and Ernestina (pp. 108–9) is couched in sentimental words ('my sweet, silly Tina') and gestures ('he knelt beside her and took her hand'). Her reaction to physical intimacy, while possibly typical of a Victorian lady, is overstated in sentimental images – 'dewy-eyed, blushing, her heart beating so fast she thought she would faint', capped by the final 'too frail for such sudden changes of emotion'.

Ernestina's and Charles's 'same insight' contrasts ironically with the understanding shared by Sarah and Charles earlier. Ernestina and

Charles seeing themselves as 'thoroughly modern young people with a thoroughly modern sense of humour' (p. 109) is also ironic. The phrase and its repetition put their 'modernity' into a broader context, simultaneously trivialising it.

Two cameo scenes are presented. First, the natural charm of the 'shy, delighted, self-surprised face' of Mary, as she tries on the dress (pp. 109–10), is offset by the voyeuristic and blasphemous thought of 'her God' perhaps wishing he were the 'Fallen One that night'. Second, at the end of Chapter 15, Charles's supercilious manner in cursorily deciding, as master, to send Sam back to London contrasts sharply with Sam's assertion 'We're not 'orses. We're 'ooman beings'. The personal sentiment and its broader socio-historical significance is poignantly enhanced by Sam's dialect (pp. 110–11).

In Chapter 16 a delay in the action is created by the tedium of a Victorian evening, as Ernestina reads a sentimental poem (pp. 112–16). The insignificant evening is dated (6 April 1867) in order to set it against an event of much greater significance that took place a week earlier, on 30 March 1867 – the Reform Bill debate.

Charles's motive for returning to the ledge in the Undercliff is given as his desire to recover a fossil. However, the narrative shift produces doubt (p. 117). The empty ledge creates tension, which is finally resolved when he sees 'a dark movement'. Sarah is compared to 'a wild animal, unable to look at him, trembling, dumb'. The image recurs, when she is seen as 'some animal at bay', her eyes flashing at Charles as if in torture (p. 121). A sudden thought of Emma Bovary comes into Charles's mind. The narrator comments 'Such allusions are comprehensions', and then significantly adds 'and temptations'. We see again the image of the 'lance' in Sarah's eyes. We are also reminded of the epigraph to Chapter 1, as Charles looks out to sea for an answer to 'this enigma'.

CHECK THE FILM

The phrase 'thoroughly modern' is repeated and draws attention to the popular musical film *Thoroughly Modern Millie*, which was released in 1967. It is another example of how Fowles integrates twentieth-century phraseology into the **narrative**.

CONTEXT

The Reform Act of 1867 enfranchised the male working classes of England and Wales. Before this Act, only one fifth of the male population could vote. Women over the age of twenty-one would wait until 1928 for full franchise, though there were several attempts over a lengthy period to gain female emancipation.

GLOSSARY

101   Periclean   Pericles (*c.* 490–429 BC), Athenian statesman, an advocate of democracy and an eloquent orator

continued

CHECK THE BOOK

For another striking example of Victorian hypocrisy and prejudice against a woman deemed to have had a disreputable past, read Anne Catherick's impassioned appeal in Chapter 8 of the 'Third Epoch' in *The Woman in White* by Wilkie Collins.

102	reginal in the manner of a queen
103	*Introit* a short prayer said as the priest goes up to the altar to celebrate Mass or Communion
104	Whigs political party that formed the core of the Liberal party in the nineteenth century
110	*Ursa bear* (Latin); Charles is mocking Sam's Cockney accent
	bargee's tool of trade, a bargepole
111	*primum mobile* the first mover (Latin)
112	*de rigueur* required by fashion (French)
113	pasha a Turkish title given to governors and high-ranking officers in the military or navy
	morocco a fine goatskin leather
114	Sheridan Richard Brinsley Sheridan (1751–1816), dramatist, politician and theatre manager
	Melbourne Lord Melbourne (1779–1848), English statesman and prime minister from 1834 to 1841; he was charged with the seduction of Mrs Norton but cleared of blame
	crim. con. abbreviation for 'criminal conversation'; in other terms, adultery
	eulogy a speech or piece of writing praising a person
	Florence Nightingale (1820–1910) known as the Lady of the Lamp, a nurse in the Crimean War and a reformer of hospital practices
115	John Stuart Mill (1806–73) English philosopher, reformer, supporter of Utilitarianism and of women's rights
	Punch satirical magazine founded in 1841
117	matrix the rock material in which fossils are embedded
118	exophthalmic abnormal protruding of the eyeball
119	Gibson Girl drawings by the American artist Charles Dana Gibson (1867–1944) created a fashionable image of the ideal female
	Lavater's *Physiognomy* Johann Kaspar Lavater (1741–1801), Swiss theologian, poet and physiognomist, who argued that the face was an indication of character
120	*Madame Bovary* a novel of 1857 by the French novelist Gustave Flaubert (1821–80), the central character of which is Emma Bovary, a woman of ordinary origins, who commits adultery before taking her own life in despair

CHAPTERS 17–18

- During a concert, Charles considers his relationship with Ernestina and their forthcoming marriage.
- Sam's relationship with Mary provides a contrast.
- Charles visits Ware Commons, but avoids the area where Sarah walks.
- Sarah appears, engages in conversation with Charles and asks that he meet her again to hear her story.

Charles, Ernestina and Mrs Tranter attend a concert. Charles reflects on his relationship with Ernestina. His thoughts turn to Sarah. He believes that marriage to Ernestina will solve his problems; however, his thoughts are not about love, but about finance and sex.

The relationship between Sam and Mary is deepening into a mutual and honest attraction.

In Chapter 18 Charles finds himself suddenly free when Ernestina has a slight migraine. He goes to Ware Commons to search for geological specimens, but decides to avoid the area where Sarah might be found. As Charles searches, Sarah appears at the entrance to a tunnel of ivy. She offers him two tests (fossil shells). Charles attempts to get away, but Sarah says that she has no one to help her. She wishes to reveal her story and suggests a further meeting. Charles agrees reluctantly. As he leaves, he considers his foolishness and the fact that he has betrayed Ernestina emotionally.

COMMENTARY

The concert (pp. 125–9) permits us to enter Charles's thoughts as he assesses his relationships with Ernestina and with Sarah. The **narrative** catches the trivialising tone ('deucedly difficult', 'in very hot water indeed') and the self-deceiving understatement ('in simple truth, he had become a little obsessed with Sarah … or at any rate with the enigma she presented'). His thoughts turn to self-pity,

> **CONTEXT**
>
> For a fine photograph of a *Micraster test* (a petrified sea urchin), see page 150 of James Aubrey's *John Fowles and Nature*.

CHECK THE BOOK

'Charles feels trapped by convention of rank and economics, and he is uncomfortably aware of the natural freedom among the lower classes – particularly their uninhibited sexuality' (Huffaker, *John Fowles*, 1980, p. 111).

somewhat overstated in the idea of 'a brilliant man trapped, a Byron tamed'. However, he is right in his perception that his future with Ernestina is now 'a fixed voyage to a known place'. His thoughts linger on three aspects in order: first sexual ('in his bed'), second financial ('in his bank'), and then, after an elliptical pause, virtually as an afterthought, romantic ('and of course in his heart, too').

The final section of Chapter 17 (pp. 129–33) provides an upstairs–downstairs contrast, the servants enjoying each other's company in their restricted social position while their superiors hide their true feeling behind a façade.

Free to visit the Undercliff, Charles's **voice**, rationalising what he is and isn't doing, strikes a hollow note: 'he had sternly forbidden himself to go anywhere near the cliff-meadow' (p. 135).

In tranquil surroundings, the 'sound as of a falling stone' alerts the reader, so that when Charles has that sixth sense of not being alone, we share the moment.

Though thoughts of the madness that Grogan later suggests (Chapter 19) cross Charles's mind, Sarah is seen as if in a painting (p. 136). Charles sees the tests (fossil shells) she gives him as a gift in return for a favour (p. 143), but the **symbolism** is seen in terms of Jungian amulets from the quester's guide, or as a sexual symbol of actual testes, which the fossil shells do, in fact, resemble.

Sarah takes the initiative, even though she is in a desperate situation. Her fate, should she go to London, is made clear. Her openness about her guilt contrasts with Charles's hypocrisy and chauvinism. He wants to escape, but Sarah's impassioned speech (pp. 139–43) holds him. Whether it is 'a litany learned by heart', and therefore a part of Sarah's plans, needs to be seen in the context of her plight and Charles's evasive responses. His concerns about 'escape from the appalling predicament he had been landed in', his appropriately capitalised 'Alarmed Propriety' and simply his concern about the threat of scandal place Charles in a poor light. Charles's masks are seen as Darwinian '*cryptic coloration*' and this 'survival by learning to blend with one's surroundings' is placed in the broader perspective of the Victorian age. Sarah's refusal to accept 'the mask, the safe distance' causes Charles to look down (pp. 143–4).

Images of danger ('a brink over an abyss'), paths (something 'wrong in his reading of the map') and sin ('he was about to engage in the forbidden, or rather the forbidden was about to engage in him') recur. Charles's turmoil is seen in his stumbling away from the encounter. He recognises 'the folly of his behaviour', yet there is no debate about whether he will tell Ernestina ('he knew he would not'). His metaphorically stepping off the Cobb and setting sail for China suggests a journey away from security and a socially accepted relationship with his fiancée.

CHECK THE BOOK

Patricia Beatty points out that the epigraph to Chapter 19 makes it clear that variation from the norm is sometimes the best means of survival: 'any being, if it vary however slightly in any manner profitable to itself, under the complex and varying conditions of life, will have a better chance of surviving, and thus be naturally selected' ('The Undercliff as Inverted Pastoral', in Aubrey, ed., *John Fowles and Nature*, p. 176).

GLOSSARY

126	**Ramadan** ninth month of the Muslim calendar, when fasting is observed from dawn to dusk
	vert espérance literally meaning green hope (French)
	pelisse a fur-trimmed cloak or coat
	Balmoral boots boots with lacings at the front
	sotto voce in an undertone or an aside (Italian)
	John-Bull-like John Bull was a symbolic figure representing England; a generic name for an Englishman
128	**Handel … Bach** George Friedrich Handel (1685–1759), German-English composer; Johann Sebastian Bach (1685–1750), German composer
129	***moue*** a pout or look of disdain (French)
	Seven Dials an area close to Covent Garden
130	**The world is only too literally too much with us now** an adapted **allusion** to a sonnet by William Wordsworth: 'The world is too much with us now; late and soon / Getting and spending, we lay waste our powers'
131	**haberdasher** a seller of small sewing articles
132	**A demang, madymosselle** Sam's attempt at the French 'à demain, mademoiselle', meaning 'until tomorrow, miss'
	Roman sign of mercy thumbs-up sign given by emperors to signify the sparing of a gladiator
133	**duenna** an elderly woman acting as a chaperone

continued

135	polypody a type of fern
	arboretum a place where trees and shrubs are grown for scientific or educational purposes
136	Gavarnie a town close to Lourdes in the Pyrenees mountains, in France, where a group of children claimed to have seen an apparition of the Virgin
	déboulis a pile of rocks
	ambulacra bands in the shell of primitive marine creature
139	litany a prayer of repeated requests
143	*cryptic coloration* in animals, a protective ability to camouflage themselves or blend in with the environment; the phrase was coined by Darwin

QUESTION

On page 140 Charles compares Sarah and himself to figures from the Greek myth of Odysseus, a warrior who had many adventures after being separated from his companions in a sea storm, and was captured and detained by the siren Calypso, a sea nymph. What does this say about Charles and his view of himself and Sarah?

CHAPTER 19

- Charles entertains Ernestina, her aunt and Dr Grogan at his hotel.
- Later Charles converses with Dr Grogan, who believes that Sarah is suffering from some form of melancholia.
- Charles and Dr Grogan express admiration for Darwin and his views.

Charles entertains Ernestina, Mrs Tranter and Dr Grogan at the White Lion, where Grogan takes over the role of host. Grogan is a bachelor, pleasant and witty in company, a man of humanity with experience of life, a lover of good food and wine, and a good raconteur.

When Grogan and Charles have escorted the ladies home, the doctor invites Charles to his house. After talk of politics and religion, the conversation is turned by Charles to the topic of Sarah. Grogan believes that she is suffering from 'melancholia' (p. 151). He expresses distaste for Mrs Poulteney's so-called piety. A colleague of his had offered Sarah a post as a governess in Exeter, but she had refused to move. Grogan says that she could be cured by a sympathetic confidante. However, he believes that Sarah does not wish to be cured and that it is a matter of waiting for her to come out of her melancholia.

Meanwhile, Sarah is pictured sharing the same bed as Millie, the servant whom she has helped. There are digressions about Victorian sexuality and the living conditions of agricultural labourers, from which group Millie come. The action moves back to Charles and Dr Grogan, who discuss palaeontology. They celebrate their common bond of belief in Darwinism.

COMMENTARY

The main purpose of this chapter is to introduce Dr Grogan, who is in many ways the voice of Victorian reason with regard to Sarah. Eccentric in some ways, a Darwinian in a Victorian society whose foundations had been shaken by the new discoveries and theories, he is presented as a sympathetic character. His views are coloured by the age in which he lives, but his assessment of Sarah and the dangers of the hysterical female offers one way that Charles can look at her motives and actions. There is a suggestion of the voyeur in Grogan, in the detail given of the telescope, the view over the bay and the bathing machines. The tongue that 'flickered wickedly out', almost serpent-like, suggests devilment, and the wink hints at a touch of salacious enjoyment (p. 148).

The cameo of Sarah sleeping with Millie is seen more as sympathy between young women caught up in a hostile environment than anything sexual. The narrator intersperses Victorian attitudes to sex with twentieth-century **allusions**, placing matters in the broader perspective of time. The relationship between Sarah and Millie is seen as tender and innocent though, as ever, the reader must decide (pp. 154–5).

The continuing conversation between Charles and Grogan (pp. 156–9) permits **ironic** comment, beginning with the men being seen as 'the two lords of creation' and Charles as 'the naturally selected', with the narrator's added ironic comment, in parentheses, about the adverb. Juxtaposition of biblical and Darwinian references encapsulates the Victorian conflict.

CHECK THE BOOK

Carol M. Barnum argues: 'Charles recognizes that Grogan's advice is intellectually sound, but he is half in love with Sarah, that half of himself which is his anima: and he is, although not in the sense Grogan intended, attempting to know himself. Grogan's advice is limited because it is based solely on reason and scientific evidence' (*The Fiction of John Fowles*, p. 58).

CONTEXT

The Gregorian telescope in Dr Grogan's study, named after James Gregory (1638–75), calls to mind mention of the telescope in Chapter 1 (p. 10), and also has a connection with the one in Fowles's own study (see fourth photograph, pp. 318–19, in Warburton, *John Fowles*, 2004).

CHECK THE BOOK

In Daniel Defoe's novel *Robinson Crusoe* (1719), Crusoe is shipwrecked alone on an island and befriended by a native whom he names Man Friday.

CONTEXT

Alongside Defoe, other important eighteenth-century figures are mentioned in this chapter: François Marie Arouet de Voltaire (1694–1778), a French author, and a leading figure in the French enlightenment in the eighteenth century, and Edmund Burke (1729–97), an Irish statesman, philosopher and political writer.

Grogan's **melodramatic** grasp of Charles's hand, 'as if he were Crusoe and Charles, Man Friday' suggests that the two men are isolated, almost 'enisled' in Victorian society and convention. In spite of Charles's seeming intellect, the chapter still leaves him and us with the cryptic mystery of Sarah.

GLOSSARY

145	**eunuchistic Hibernian** in the manner of an Irishman with a lack of sexual interest in women
146	*comme il faut* as it should be, correct and proper (French)
147	*souffrante* suffering (French)
	Hoffmann's Tales Ernst Theodor Hoffmann (1776–1822), German writer, whose Tales are the inspiration for Offenbach's opera *Tales of Hoffmann*
	Prince Consort Prince Albert (1819–61), husband of Queen Victoria
	Dulce est desipere it is pleasant to cast aside serious thought (Latin); from the Odes of Horace, an ancient Roman poet (12:24)
148	**nereids** sea nymphs
	bathing-machines huts that could be wheeled into the sea, enabling Victorian ladies to enter the water in a decorous manner
	Burmah cheroot, a cigar
149	*Quisque suos patimur manes* from Virgil, *The Aeneid*, Book VI: 'Each one must suffer his own spirits of the dead'; Grogan's admittedly free translation is in the text
	Bentham Jeremy Bentham (1748–1832), English philosopher and law reformer
	Parian marble from the Greek island of Paros
	Vital Religion a philosophical doctrine that expresses belief in a metaphysical soul
	Matthew Arnold (1822–88) English poet and educationist
	neo-ontologist a new follower of a branch of metaphysics that deals with the nature of pure being
150	**Augustan** referring to the period of elegance in literature and the arts during the eighteenth century, and named after the Roman emperor Augustus, whose reign was characterised by such style

151	**Bedlam** a corruption of Bethlehem, the London asylum for lunatics
152	**jarvey** driver of a hackney coach
	Doctor Hartmann Eduard von Hartmann (1842–1906), German philosopher who wrote about the human mind, particularly the unconscious
	Weimar a city and state in east central Germany
154	**anathema** an object of abhorrence
155	**chlorotic** affected by chlorosis, a wasting disease particularly in young woman
	Eggardon a hill-fort near Bridport in Dorset
	George Morland (1763–1804) English painter of rural scenes and subjects
	Birket Foster (1825–99) English landscape painter
	Happy Swain the happy country peasant
	Versailles the palace outside Paris, residence of the kings of France from 1682 to 1789
156	**Buffon … _Époques de la Nature_** the Compte de Buffon (1707–88), French naturalist
157	**Archbishop Ussher** James Ussher (1581–1656) was Archbishop of Armagh in Ireland
	camphine an old name for turpentine, a flammable oil
158	**Gosse** Philip Henry Gosse (1810–88), English naturalist and biologist
	bas-bleu blue-stocking (French)
	carbonari members of an Italian secret society in early nineteenth-century Naples, who sought to establish a republican government in Italy

CHAPTERS 20–1

- Charles meets Sarah, who confesses her involvement with the French lieutenant.
- Charles tries to persuade her to leave Lyme.
- Hidden from view, Charles and Sarah see Sam and Mary kissing in the clearing.

QUESTION

Read the two epigraphs to Chapter 20 carefully. What is suggested here about the conflict between God and Nature?

Charles enters the clearing through the tunnel of ivy. Sarah has watched him approaching. She offers him another test (fossil shell). Charles recalls Grogan's words and justifies his presence here as scientific and humanitarian. He dismisses telling Ernestina about the encounters.

Sarah leads him through another tunnel. He follows her to a dell surrounded by brambles and carpeted with flowers. They are silent for some time. Charles attempts to get Sarah to reveal her story. She tells of Varguennes's injuries and his recovery. She now knows that all he had said to her was untrue. At the time, however, she was attracted to him. She tells of her happiness as governess at Mrs Talbot's. Sarah says that Varguennes had asked her to accompany him to France, with talk of marriage. After first rejecting the idea, she eventually followed him to Weymouth, where he waited for her. She realised that he was false, but she sacrificed herself to him.

The effect of Sarah's confession causes Charles to consider a mythical world of beauty and truth. As he considers a romantic escape, Charles sees the image of his dead sister ahead of him.

The confession continues. Varguennes admitted he was married and Sarah realised that she wanted never to see him again. This is the first time she has ever told anyone. She expresses the desire to be seen as an outcast. Charles cannot understand this and suggests that she must leave Lyme. Eventually Sarah agrees. As they are talking, they hear voices. Sarah moves into the shadows, beckoning Charles to follow. They see Sam and Mary kissing on the grassy bank. Charles is embarrassed and looks at Sarah, who smiles. In the smile, Charles senses danger and declares that they must never meet again. As Sam and Mary leave, Charles and Sarah remain silent before they depart separately. Charles sees the 'old lancing look' (p. 182) before she moves off down through the trees.

COMMENTARY

Charles's meeting with Sarah takes place in the shadowy tunnel of ivy, while outside the natural world is brilliant and full of natural life. A vivid image of Charles accompanied by 'swarms of spring butterflies' contrasts with the adverb 'nefariously' that describes

CHECK THE BOOK

John Fowles writes: 'In the wood I know best there is a dell among beeches at the foot of a chalk cliff. Not a person a month goes there now, since it is well away from any path … There are freedoms in the woods that our ancestors perhaps realised more fully than we do. I used this wood, and even this particular dell, in *The French Lieutenant's Woman*, for scenes that it seemed to me in a story of self-liberation, could have no other setting' (*The Tree*, 1979, pp. 74–5).

Charles's entry into 'the dark-green shade beneath the ivy' (p. 160). The gift of another test, like 'some expiatory offering', seems to further bind Charles to Sarah.

The narrative shift expresses Charles's 'clear element of duty', based on 'a scientific as well as a humanitarian reason' (p. 161). It is expressed in Darwinian terms as the duty of 'the *human* fittest' with a responsibility towards 'the less fit'.

The movement to a secluded place, through 'yet another green tunnel', takes Charles further into Sarah's domain (p. 162). Images of pathways and danger and falling are woven into the narrative before we come to the hidden dell. Its natural beauty, with 'primroses and violets', 'the white stars of wild strawberries', is offset by images of 'dense thickets of brambles and dogwood' and a 'stunted thorn tree'. Again, the Pre-Raphaelite iconography is apparent.

Sarah's fragmented history is expanded by her account of the Varguennes affair. She concludes her story with a brutally realistic view, saying, 'I am nothing. I am hardly human any more. I am the French Lieutenant's Whore' (p. 171). However, in spite of a bleak future, she has 'a freedom they cannot understand'.

Charles recognises the **ambiguity** of his forgiveness for her 'unchastity' and his glimpse into 'the dark shadows where he might have enjoyed it himself'. In the imagined romantic landscape of 'towers and ramparts', there is a disturbing psychological figure – 'a dark shadow, his dead sister' moving ahead of him (p. 173). This juxtaposition of the dead sister with the idyllic romance is explained in Jungian terms by some critics.

The smile that Sarah shares with Charles as they see Sam and Mary enjoying simple sexual pleasure is seen as a challenge to Victorian pretensions as well as being a moment of Charles's incomplete understanding of Sarah (p. 179). The image of the man coming to a 'sought-for door ... but only to find it locked' further suggests this. Again, we find images of a fall ('precipice', 'plunge') that lead Charles to the brink of 'a passionate reciprocity of feeling' (p. 180).

QUESTION

How is Sarah seen as more liberated here, in spite of her difficult circumstances?

CHECK THE BOOK

Patricia Beatty points to a Jungian explanation of 'the transfiguration of the image of Sarah into that of Charles's sister' ('The Undercliff as Inverted Pastoral: The Fowlesian *Felix Culpa* in *The French Lieutenant's Woman*', in Aubrey, ed., *John Fowles and Nature*, p. 174).

CHECK THE BOOK

Suzanne Ross comments on Sarah's connection with the natural world in '"Water out of a Woodland Spring": Sarah Woodruff and Nature in *The French Lieutenant's Woman*'. The essay is in Aubrey's *John Fowles and Nature*, pp. 188–94.

The incongruity of the 'old lancing look' and the adverb 'lightly' that describes Sarah's movement through the trees reinforces the enigma (p. 182).

GLOSSARY

163	**eyries** the nests of eagles
164	*demi-monde* the shady and unrespectable classes; often applied to women
167	**patrimony** inheritance from a father or from ancestors
	Unionists members or advocates of trade unions
170	**the devil's instrument** censorious Victorian term for the wine Sarah had drunk earlier
172	**claustrophilia** love of enclosed spaces, the opposite of claustrophobia
	Ford Madox Brown (1821–93) English painter and writer
	Constable John Constable (1776–1837), English landscape painter
	Palmer Samuel Palmer (1805–81), English landscape painter
173	**Thélème** in François Rabelais's *Gargantua*, an abbey built as a place of total freedom and pleasure
	Mohammedan westernised term of reference for a follower of Islam, here used in a Victorian prejudiced and derogatory sense
	Tyrrhenian the sea off the western coast of Italy, part of the Mediterranean
	Avila city and province of central Spain
	ashlar a block of cut stone
179	*in flagrante delicto* in the very act, usually of sexual intercourse (Latin)
185	**grand vizir** a head minister or councillor in the Muslim states
	Carolean belonging to the time of Charles I (1600–49) or his son Charles II (1630–85)
	Gobelins tapestries from the Paris factory and dye works founded by the Gobelin family in about 1450
	Claudes works by Claude Lorrain (c. 1600–82), French landscape artist

185	Tintoretto Jacopo Robusti (1518–94), Venetian artist, the son of a dyer – hence his Italian nickname, which means 'the little dyer'
187	Crystal Palace a building of glass and iron erected for the Great Exhibition in Hyde Park, London, in 1851

CHAPTERS 22–4

- Charles decides to end his involvement with Sarah.
- He returns to Lyme, where he receives a telegram from his uncle requesting his presence.
- Charles goes to Winsyatt full of hope, anticipating good news.
- Sarah, meanwhile, allows herself to be seen by Mrs Fairley on Ware Commons.
- Charles tells Ernestina about his uncle's plans to marry.
- Sarah has been dismissed by Mrs Poulteney, and has disappeared.

QUESTION

What do you note about Charles's thoughts and reactions in these three chapters? How do they compare to those of Ernestina?

On his way back to Lyme in Chapter 22, Charles considers his dangerous situation. He decides to end the relationship with Sarah and place matters in the hands of Mrs Tranter. A telegram awaiting him from his uncle requests an urgent visit to Winsyatt. Charles thinks that his uncle may be considering offering him the manor house or the slightly smaller property in the village. He tells Ernestina of this. She urges Charles to seek the manor house. She plans to get rid of the period furniture and the paintings in the house and replace them with modern furnishings.

As Charles enters Winsyatt in Chapter 23, he notices that there are new curtains and carpets. The stuffed bustard has gone. Meanwhile, on her way back to Lyme from the earlier rendezvous with Charles Sarah has been seen by Mrs Fairley, who is at the Dairy.

In Chapter 24 Charles tells Ernestina that his uncle is to marry a younger widow. This news has shocked Charles and it clearly alters

CHECK THE BOOK

An early nineteenth-century novel with themes of inheritance and differing attitudes to modernity and tradition is Jane Austen's *Mansfield Park* (1814).

CHECK THE NET

Charles seems to be falling back into the attitudes of the traditional Victorian gentleman. For further ideas about the 'gentleman' in the Victorian age, visit **www. victorianweb.org** and click on 'Social History', then 'Race, Class and Gender Issues', and go to 'The Gentleman'.

his inheritance prospects. Ernestina's bitter outburst alarms him even more. A further shock for Charles is that Sarah has been dismissed by Mrs Poulteney, and this disappearance causes concern for her safety.

COMMENTARY

Charles is confident that he has successfully dealt with the situation concerning Sarah. The voice from his sensibilities (pp. 183–4) expresses variously a sense of relief ('his folly had not been visited on him'), self-assurance ('he was one of the fittest') and a rather patronising, chauvinistic view of Sarah ('A remarkable young woman, a remarkable young woman'). His certainty that the matter is over is conveyed through the excessive repetition of 'free will', though the very fact of this repetition suggests some doubt about his confidence.

The narrator comments on two of Sarah's qualities that Charles may have overlooked – 'passion and imagination'. Charles stands as representative of his age when he dismisses them from the equation, the former being seen as 'sensuality' and the latter as 'merely fanciful' (p. 184).

The telegram from Charles's uncle provides an excuse for him to avoid the dilemma of deceiving Ernestina by 'further lies of omission'; there is the **ironic** comment that 'family had come to his aid' (p. 184). Sarah is seen mistakenly by Charles at this point as 'an object of his past'. The expectation of inheritance lifts Charles's spirits, while Ernestina reveals her middle-class values by dismissing the traditional trappings and values of Winsyatt. The adverbs and possessive pronouns that colour her tone are italicised for emphasis (p. 185). Beneath it all, however, there lurks a fear that she is moving out of her class.

Ernestina's plans for refurbishment and Charles's confidence that he can manoeuvre his uncle into letting him have either one of his properties show both of them in a poor light – in Ernestina's case with regard to taste and in Charles's with regard to gratitude.

The idea that Charles is moving into his rightful place in society and the traditional order that Winsyatt represents is conveyed in the first four pages of Chapter 23. It is seen as 'this piece of England' which 'belonged to him, and he belonged to it'. Charles sees the moment as the rather ironically expressed 'call to the throne' and at the same time, significantly, dismisses 'the absurd adventure in the Undercliff' with Sarah.

Charles's confidence, however, is underpinned by misread signals. He fails to see the significance of the 'empty hall', 'the new curtains' and carpets and the disappearance of the ironically named 'immortal bustard' (p. 192).

The scene changes, and we see Sarah leaving the woods and heading towards the Dairy. The narrator refuses to let us enter Sarah's mind, though her intentions seem clear in her bold move into full view of Mrs Fairley. In Victorian episodic and **melodramatic** fashion, the reader is invited to anticipate the outcome.

The other cliff-hanger, 'still he did not guess' in the middle of Chapter 23, is answered in Chapter 24. We begin with repeated reactions from Ernestina ('monstrous …') in response to the breaking of the news that the uncle is to marry, thereby probably depriving Charles of inheritance and title. Ernestina's sentiments (pp. 194–6) reveal 'the draper's daughter' in her, a lack of the 'imperturbability' that would have been present in the upper classes.

Dramatic news then reveals that Sarah has been dismissed and is missing. This brings back the problems that had seemed to diminish with the first news from Winsyatt and Charles's 'free-willing' himself to a secure position. He is the only one to know where Sarah will be found. This knowledge 'oppressed him like a shroud', a subliminal reference to the **motif** of the dead woman that has previously appeared in the supposed 'corpse' (p. 73) and will recur in the encounter in Carslake's barn (p. 235). The final 'thunder in the offing' (p. 198) is an example of **pathetic fallacy** and suggests ominous developments.

CHECK THE BOOK

It has been suggested that *The French Lieutenant's Woman* bears similarities to Charles Dickens's *Great Expectations*, not only in the theme of expectations but also in the growth to understanding of the hero, the romantic quest for the distant woman and the alternative endings.

QUESTION

Read the final section of Chapter 23 (pp. 192–3), where you have to decide what is going on in Sarah's mind. What do you notice about Sarah's decision? Think about the path image, the consequences of her move and the narrative point of view.

GLOSSARY

189	chaise a light open carriage for one or two people
	calash the folding top of a carriage
	Baucis in Greek mythology, the wife of Philemon; the couple were noted for their hospitality to Zeus and Hermes
190	fenestrated having spots where the light passes through
	billycock a hard felt hat
191	seigneurially in the manner of a seigneur or feudal lord
	Palladian in the neo-classical style of architecture of the Italian Andrea Palladio (1508–80)
192	the younger Wyatt Sir Matthew Digby Wyatt (1820–77), an English architect

CHECK THE BOOK

Hardy, in *A Pair of Blue Eyes*, has a moment similar to Charles's realisation about history and life. Knight, like Charles a geologist, is clinging precariously to a rock face when he sees in the rock a fossil and has an understanding of time which 'closed up like a fan before him. He saw himself at one extremity of the years, face to face with the beginning and all the intermediate centuries simultaneously' (Chapter 22).

CHAPTERS 25–6

- Charles receives two notes from Sarah, one of which is seen by Sam.
- Sam's thoughts turn towards blackmail.
- In a flashback we hear of the meeting between Charles and his uncle, whose marriage alters Charles's expectations of inheritance.

Charles intends to send a message to Grogan about assisting in the search for Sarah. Before he can do this, he finds on his table a note sealed with black wax. It is from Sarah, requesting one final meeting. Charles is angry that she should put him at risk by sending a note. Sam is sent to find out who brought the note. Charles recalls the blue lias rock containing ammonites and has a sudden insight that history is not vertical but horizontal. Sam tells him that the messenger was a small boy. As Charles looks out of the window, he sees a boy approaching the hotel.

The boy delivers another note from Sarah, and this time Sam knows that it is from her. Sam is told to keep the matter to himself. Charles says that he has planned to find Sarah a situation and that he will reveal all to Mrs Tranter. The note, in French, tells that she has waited all day for Charles and that she will wait for him at the barn by the farm on Ware Commons.

As the storm breaks, Charles decides to go out as he needs to 'lay bare his soul' (p. 202) to someone. He passes Sam on the stairs.

In Chapter 26 Sam's thoughts reveal that he is ambitious to enter the drapery business. His thoughts also turn to the knowledge he has about Charles and Sarah.

In a flashback, the **narrative** details the meeting between Charles and his uncle. Charles's reaction to news of the marriage is 'stiffly polite'. The uncle provides detail of his courtship of Mrs Tomkins. He acknowledges the change in Charles's fortunes, but offers, as a wedding gift, the smaller house in the village for as long as Charles lives. There is an implicit rebuke to Charles about his neglect of the lonely old uncle; the older servants at Winsyatt perceive this neglect and Charles's careless lifestyle.

Some of the changes at Winsyatt brought about by Mrs Tomkins are mentioned. Charles's uncle shows him a miniature of Mrs Tomkins's face in a locket. Charles notes a slight resemblance to Sarah. He also sees in the portrait a strong woman. As Charles leaves Winsyatt, his thoughts are sad. The weather and the landscape seem also to have changed.

Charles thinks of Ernestina and the fact that his uncle had not been impressed by her middle-class origins. Ernestina's large dowry is possibly seen by the uncle as some relief for Charles, as his own fortunes now are tied to Mrs Tomkins. Charles feels inferior to Ernestina in financial standing.

 **QUESTION**

In what way do Sam's aspirations on page 204 foreshadow later events in his life and changes in Victorian society?

COMMENTARY

Events have unfolded on two different fronts: Charles's visit to Winsyatt, and Sarah's deliberate decision to let Mrs Fairley see her on Ware Commons, thereby causing her dismissal from Mrs Poulteney's. Charles knows where Sarah will be found, though knowledge of his connection with her is now in dangerous hands. The aside about Sam's aspirations develops the social theme of the rising working classes and also Sam's distaste for his master beneath his 'mask of manservitude' (p. 201). The earlier thunder, and now the 'distant flash of lightning' heralding the coming of a storm, match the growing tensions in Charles's life. The dark clouds that envelop Charles (p. 202) are seen in both the literal and the metaphorical sense. The tension is conveyed not only in Charles's thoughts, but also in his sharp words and his wild actions. The narrator intervenes with a comment about 'overdoing the exclamation marks'. This, however, does not detract from the pace of the action in Chapter 25.

The epiphany that Charles experiences occurs in 'a flash of black lightning' (p. 200), which is appropriate as the sudden realisation that time is horizontal comes just as actual lightning is heralding the approaching storm. His understanding of time reveals the reality of the 'now' and the illusory nature of those cornerstones of the Victorian age – 'history, religion, duty, social position'.

The flashback of Chapter 26 (pp. 207–12) explains Ernestina's anger at the start of Chapter 24, and the signs in Chapter 23 that Charles saw but did not comprehend are now fully explained. The conversation with his uncle (pp. 207–11) is conducted in gentlemanly terms, though **narrative** shifts enable the reader to move between the sensibilities of the two. The suggestion that Mrs Tomkins has seen an advantageous liaison with his uncle lies in the **subtext** of Charles's thoughts. The comparison of the acquisition of the new 'brood-mare' and Mrs Tomkins, the widow young enough to bear children, is perhaps more than subtext.

Charles's departure (p. 211) is in sharp contrast to his arrival three or four hours earlier (pp. 189–92). The optimism that caused him to see the Winsyatt estate as a 'fortunate destiny and right order' is now overcast, literally with 'a high veil of cirrus' and also figuratively with Charles's corresponding thoughts of 'morose introspection'. The consideration 'if he had never met Ernestina in the first place …' is left incomplete, but Charles's dark thought is implicit in the ellipsis (p. 212). Moreover, by the narrator's

CONTEXT

The intervention by the narrator here is an **alienation** technique. Charles's thoughts have formed the main part of the narrative. Now the reader is distanced from the narrative and invited to take a critical view of Charles's 'acute and self-directed anxiety' (p. 202).

QUESTION

These two chapters employ narrative shifts involving Charles, his uncle and Sam. Read closely to detect these shifts. What effects are created? Consider language, voice, tone and the differences between what is said and what is thought.

manipulation of time we have already witnessed Ernestina's reaction to the news, and this further alienates her from Charles.

GLOSSARY

199	Abernethy biscuits hard biscuits, originally flavoured with caraway
203	gasolier a hanging frame with gas jets to provide light
204	samovar an elaborately decorated Russian urn for boiling water or making tea
205	taproom a room in an inn where beer is served from the tap in a cask
206	ant's-eye view of the frivolous grasshopper 'The ant and the grasshopper' is a fable by Aesop, in which the hard-working ant is shown to be superior as a survivor to the frivolous, lazy grasshopper
	imprimatur let it be printed (Latin); hence permission to print a book
	ducatur in matrimonium let he or she be led into matrimony (Latin); hence a permission to marry
	faute de mieux for want of a better alternative (French)
207	niminy-piminy affectedly fine or delicate
208	bullfinch a high, thick hedge, hard to jump over
209	Joe Manton Joseph Manton (1760–1835), a noted manufacturer of sporting guns
211	*rentier* someone living on a fixed income, or on income from investments (French)

CHAPTERS 27–8

- Charles visits Dr Grogan, who assesses Sarah's motives.
- Grogan advises Charles to stay with Ernestina.
- He gives Charles the transcript of a French court case that involved a hysterical woman.
- Charles reads the transcript and goes out to find Sarah.

CONTEXT

An article entitled 'The Modern Governess System', published in *Fraser's Magazine* 30, November 1844, states, 'The statistics touching lunatic asylums give a frightful proportion of governesses in the list of the insane.'

Chapter 27 picks up the story from Chapter 25, when Charles rushed out of the hotel. He goes to Dr Grogan's house, where the doctor supposes the confidential talk will be on sexual matters, either about some disease or possibly ignorance. When Grogan mentions Sarah's disappearance after her dismissal, Charles declares that this is why he has come. Grogan believes Charles's reason is connected with the search, but Charles reveals his involvement.

Grogan uses a copy of *On the Origin of Species* as a replacement for the Bible to indicate confidentiality between the two men. He advises that Charles has been deceived into a compromising situation and suggests that Charles should meet Sarah and arrange a placement for her in a private asylum. He gives Charles a transcript of a court case in France that involved a hysterical young woman and a young officer.

Chapter 28 primarily comprises the account of the Lieutenant de La Roncière trial, with some references to psychiatric histories of hysteria in women. The case shocks Charles. His thoughts turn to Sarah and he begins to doubt his trust in Dr Grogan. He decides to go to meet Sarah.

Commentary

Grogan's musings about Charles's visit to discuss 'private and very personal' matters reveal some Victorian sexual problems and misconceptions. When Sarah is mentioned Grogan again makes the wrong assumption, thinking that Charles's visit is due to anxiety over her disappearance (pp. 213–14).

Grogan swears confidence, somewhat dramatically, on a copy of *On the Origin of Species*, as if it were a Bible. This image encapsulates the dispute between Darwinism and religion.

Along with the epigraphs that direct the reader, the literary sources from Grogan and the footnotes play with **intertextuality** in order to disorientate the reader. The account of the Lieutenant de La Roncière case, the conviction of an innocent man on the basis of spurious evidence, and the material from Matthaie on his innocence and on female hysteria shock Charles. However, the absolute

CHECK THE BOOK

There is a suggestion that Sarah is to Dr Grogan 'another text, a case study of an unbalanced woman. In fact, he turns her literally into a text by presenting Charles with the medical documents pertaining to a similar case revolving around another young French officer, a Lieutenant de La Roncière, falsely charged with raping the daughter of his commanding officer. Grogan attempts to explain Sarah's behaviour in terms of Marie, the girl in the case study' (Thomas C. Foster, *Understanding John Fowles*, p. 81).

innocence of the lieutenant is queried by a 1968 study of judicial errors, referred to in the footnote on page 229. If Clough's views (p. 223) about the assumptions of science are valid, then the medical advice of Grogan and Matthaie may be false. However, pulling in a different direction, the Arnold epigraph at the beginning of Chapter 28 advising against springing to judgement takes the reader and Charles back to God, the final judge.

The questions asked of the reader are about relative truth, and there is no definitive answer in the text. The novel's **ludic subversion** works on serious matters such as guilt and innocence, truth and deceit, interpretation and misinterpretation – throughout all of which operates the idea of time.

Charles's dilemma (pp. 230–1) runs through a confusion of thoughts about his own actions and decisions, about the advice he has been given, about Sarah, about destiny. It is with this last thought that he makes a decision to go to Sarah regardless of the consequences: 'if he met Grogan, he met him'.

CHECK THE BOOK

Christopher Bigsby's excellent interview with John Fowles, in which the author talks of many issues in this phase of *The French Lieutenant's Woman*, can be found in *The Radical Imagination and the Liberal Tradition: Interviews with English and American Novelists*, 1982, pp. 114–25; reprinted in Dianne L. Vipond, ed., *Conversations with John Fowles*, 1999, pp. 70–81.

GLOSSARY

216	Samaritan the good Samaritan helped the injured stranger by the roadside (see Luke 10: 29–37)
217	*in extremis* in extreme circumstances (Latin)
	de profundis out of the depths (Latin)
	de altis from the heights (Latin)
218	'I am cast out …' an adaptation, or possibly a deliberate misquotation, by Dr Grogan of the Old Testament, Jonah 2:4
	Socrates (469–399 BC) influential Greek philosopher, the tutor of Plato; convicted for supposedly corrupting the youth of Athens, he refused to pay a fine, refused to escape when given the chance and was eventually sentenced to death by drinking poison
	Malthus Thomas Malthus (1766–1834), English political economist
219	catechism a set of teachings, often set out as a series of questions and answers

continued

QUESTION

What is revealed on pages 230–1 of Charles's thoughts and situation? Look closely at the narrative, syntax, language and **allusions**.

CONTEXT

Three important French writers of the nineteenth century are mentioned in Chapter 28: Victor Hugo (1802–85), a poet, dramatist and novelist, a leader in the French Romantic movement, famous for *Les Miserables* (1862), a sweeping view of French social history; Honoré de Balzac (1799–1850), a novelist famous for the series of novels *La Comedie Humaine* (*The Human Comedy*); and George Sand, the pseudonym of Amandine Aurore Lucie Dupin, Baronne Dudevant (1804–76), a prolific female novelist.

223	martinet a strict disciplinarian
	mess place where a group of officers take their meals
224	night-chemise night dress
225	Cayenne capital city of French Guiana, South America
227	catheter an artificial tube for removing gases or liquids from the body
228	*cette adroite trompeuse* this clever deceiver (French)
	Lüneburg city and district of Germany
	Lentin Jacob Friedrich Ludwig Lentin (d. 1803), German doctor with interests in animal magnetism, phrenology and psychiatry
229	*perfide Albion* perfidious Albion (French); i.e. treacherous England
230	tautology use of words which repeat something already implied in the same statement
	Sir Galahad in the Athurian legend Sir Galahad, the noblest and purest of the Knights of the Round Table, sought the Holy Grail
	Guinevere Queen Guinevere, the faithless wife of Arthur, whom she betrayed by taking Sir Lancelot as a lover
230	Pontius Pilate Roman governor of Palestine, who sanctioned the crucifixion of Jesus (see Matthew 27:24)

CHAPTER 29

- Charles sets out for the Undercliff to meet Sarah.
- He makes his way through the woods and eventually enters the barn, fearful of what he will see.

Charles sets out early to meet Sarah in the Undercliff. The early morning atmosphere and the surroundings are pleasant, but Charles feels excluded from the idyllic scene of natural beauty. The call of a wren on a bramble bush astonishes him. He takes the path to Carslake's barn but cannot find Sarah. In the barn, he sees a black bonnet and hears a sound. He looks fearfully over the partition of a stall.

COMMENTARY

This chapter has a number of linguistic patterns, ranging from the idyllic, romanticised and natural ('a green sweetness', 'the trees dense with singing birds') to a more hostile animal imagery ('like a man going through a jungle renowned for its tigers'), and culminating in the language of **Gothic** horror ('sudden dread', 'icy premonition', 'worm-eaten planks' and 'an ominously slaked vampire'). Attention is focused on the 'tiny wren', which is seen as 'the Announcing Angel of evolution' (p. 233). Charles senses the 'ennui of human reality', in contrast to the triumph of the wren's singing. This reaction can be seen as a half-perceived epiphany in Charles's awakening understanding. He feels excluded from the ecstasy of the spiritual moment, which is described in religious terms as a 'eucharist' and a 'paradise' from which he is 'excommunicated' (p. 234).

As Charles enters the barn, he senses that he will find 'a corpse', which connects with the previous occasion when he supposed Sarah dead (Chapter 10). The unfolding of the cliff-hanger ending, as Charles peers 'fearfully over the partition', is deliberately delayed until Chapter 30.

GLOSSARY	
232	**undertaker's mute** a funeral attendant hired as a silent mourner
	sheepstealer's adage a proverb that justifies the compounding of criminal activity; various forms, including 'You might as well be hung for the sheep as for the lamb'
233	**druid** a priest in the ancient Celtic religion
	pomona apple-green
	elegiac in the form of a poem or song of mourning
	bestiary an illustrated book of animals
	Announcing Angel in the Bible, the angel Gabriel gave the news of the Messiah to Mary
234	**ennui** boredom
	pseudo-Linnaean a fake or false follower of the theory of the chain of being propounded by Linnaeus

 CHECK THE BOOK

Gothic literature, popular in the Victorian era, combined elements of horror and romance. An early satirical reaction to the Gothic is seen in Jane Austen's *Northanger Abbey* (1818). Famous examples of the Gothic can be seen in Mary Wollstonecraft Shelley's *Frankenstein* (1818) and later in the century in Bram Stoker's *Dracula* (1897).

 CHECK THE POEM

Hardy's poem 'The Darkling Thrush' contains a moment similar to the wren's triumphant call, from which the human being feels isolated (*Collected Poems*, ed. James Gibson, 2001, poem 119).

> 234   eucharist a Christian celebration of thanksgiving
>
> Greek chorus in Greek tragedy, the group of actors who commentated on the action of the drama

CHAPTER 30

- The action resumes from Sarah's return to Mrs Poulteney's, after Mrs Fairley has seen her again on Ware Commons.
- Mrs Fairley is sent to summon Sarah to a meeting with Mrs Poulteney.
- Sarah is dismissed, but she responds defiantly.

 CHECK THE BOOK

The first novel of Anne Brontë, *Agnes Grey* (1847), was written largely in response to the desperate position of the governess in the Victorian age. Unmarried, educated young women often found that the only respectable opportunity for them was as a governess. Often this was a position where exploitation, class, materialism and patriarchalism left them badly disadvantaged and facing an uncertain future.

We go back to Chapter 23, where Sarah had returned to Mrs Poulteney's just before Mrs Fairley arrived with news of having seen Sarah on Ware Commons. Mrs Fairley tells Sarah that Mrs Poulteney is waiting to speak to her downstairs. Mrs Poulteney gives Sarah a month's wages and orders her to leave.

Sarah demands to know the reason. This infuriates Mrs Poulteney, who threatens Sarah with the asylum because of the public scandal she has brought about. Accusing Mrs Poulteney of hypocrisy, Sarah leaves. She refuses the money she is offered and tells Mrs Poulteney to buy 'some instrument of torture' to torment anyone else unfortunate enough to come under her power.

Sarah's final remark about the uncertainty of Mrs Poulteney's salvation strikes home. Mrs Poulteney collapses into a chair in a feigned swoon. Sarah returns to her room, looks into the mirror and weeps.

COMMENTARY

A chronological shift takes the **narrative** back to Chapter 23. In the interim Mrs Fairley, revelling in her role as spy, has reported Sarah's presence on Ware Commons to Mrs Poulteney. Neither Mrs Fairley nor Mrs Poulteney has realised that being seen was deliberate on Sarah's part.

Mrs Poulteney's pose is seen **ironically** in terms of regality. She is not on her usual throne and is seen as 'this freezing majesty', who speaks as if she were royalty: 'I *command* you to leave this room at once' (p. 237). Sarah shows that she can play Mrs Poulteney at her own game and wins the battle of face-to-face communication, being just as determined as her mistress in her spirited challenges to the authority of the Victorian age.

Sarah strikes first at Mrs Poulteney's hypocrisy, refusing the money with the barbed instruction for Mrs Poulteney to use it for 'some instrument of torture'. The final blow strikes at the heart of Mrs Poulteney's hopes of salvation. Sarah's comment about the uncertainty of her mistress having the ear of God in the afterlife is accompanied by 'a very small, but a knowing and a telling smile' (p. 238). Sarah's only other smile has been the one she gave Charles in the tunnel of ivy (pp. 180–1). The smile in each case seems to be accompanied by understanding, and Sarah's ability to see through a mask.

The closing moment shows Sarah as vulnerable, as she kneels and weeps. The narrator, however, refuses to let us into her thoughts, other than through the enigmatic 'What she saw she could not bear'. The reader is left with the final puzzle of Sarah's belief that she was praying.

QUESTION

Compare the two smiles that Sarah gives, here on page 238 and earlier on pages 180–1. What does each incident reveal about Sarah?

CHECK THE BOOK

Once again we see Sarah's actions without being allowed into her deeper thoughts. Magali Cornier Michael comments: 'Because Sarah's point of view remains absent from the text, Sarah remains objectified and never becomes a subject in her own right' ('"Who is Sarah?" A Critique of *The French Lieutenant's Woman*'s Feminism', in *Critique: Studies in Modern Fiction* 28: 4, Summer 1987).

GLOSSARY		
236	verjuice	the sour juice of unripe fruit
237	Parthian shaft	a parting shot; the Parthians of ancient Persia used to fire arrows at pursuers by turning around in the saddle
238	Jezebel	a wicked, scheming woman or a shameless, painted woman; from Jezebel in the Bible's Books of Kings
238	sal volatile	smelling salts, used to revive someone from a faint

CHECK THE BOOK

Elizabeth Rankin suggests that the 'deeper and stranger reality' that Charles perceives in the song of the wren (pp. 233–4) 'is of course, Sarah, and for a while it seems as if she may win Charles over. … The moment, however, is only a brief one and Charles reacts to his lapse with typical revulsion' ('Cryptic Coloration in *The French Lieutenant's Woman*', p. 200).

- Charles finds Sarah sleeping in the barn and she tells him the truth about allowing Mrs Fairley to see her.
- They embrace, but Charles pushes her away and rushes to the door.
- Ernestina resolves to be submissive to Charles.
- Sam tells Mary that he is leaving Lyme with Charles.
- Sam and Mary have seen Charles coming out of the barn – Charles offers Sam money, which he refuses.
- Charles provides Sarah with money, persuading her to go to Exeter.
- Charles tells Ernestina that he must tell her father of his change in circumstances, and leaves, giving Mary a coin for her silence about Carslake's barn.

In Chapter 31 Charles finds Sarah sleeping in the barn. His first reaction is to escape, but at the door he calls out her name. Sarah awakes and Charles faces her. Sarah reveals the truth that she had deliberately allowed Mrs Fairley to see her on Ware Commons. For a moment they embrace, but Charles pushes Sarah away and runs out of the door.

The action shifts in Chapter 32 to Ernestina, who after the differences of opinion with Charles in Chapter 24 confides in her diary her intention of subjecting herself to his wishes. Sam tells Mary of the orders he has had from Charles to prepare to leave Lyme. Mary is distressed, and Mrs Tranter allows her some time off to spend with Sam.

The flashback reveals that it was Sam and Mary who were approaching the barn as Charles left. Charles tries to explain and offers Sam money, but Sam recognises this as a bribe and refuses to accept. Charles returns to the barn and provides Sarah with money, persuading her to leave Lyme and go to Exeter.

Charles calls on Ernestina. News has already reached her that he is to go to London. Ernestina is annoyed, but Charles explains that it is his duty to tell her father of his change in circumstances. He promises to deliver a letter from Ernestina to her father. As Charles leaves with a restrained embrace, he is held back by Ernestina, whom he reluctantly kisses on the lips. For a moment he feels sexual desire, but then he recalls the kiss with Sarah. Charles meets Mary, to whom he gives a gold coin, a reminder to her to keep their earlier encounter secret.

COMMENTARY

This is not the first occasion on which Charles has come across Sarah sleeping (see pp. 73–5). Again there is a conflict of emotions, as he feels the desire to possess and the desire to protect. The tension as he leaves is immediately broken by his uttering her name twice. Charles senses a natural wildness about Sarah and compares this to the song of the wren. It becomes clear that there is a mutual attraction between them. Before they embrace, the focus is on Sarah's eyes, here described as 'drowning'. Charles's reaction, as he casts aside Victorian conventions ('the moment overcame the age'), is expressed in a quick series of descriptors – 'violently', 'agonized', 'debased', 'abominable', culminating in the 'horror' (p. 243). The other 'horror', however, leaves Chapter 31 on a **melodramatic** cliff-hanger, which is not resolved until Chapter 33.

The intervening chapter shifts to Ernestina, who has passed a disturbed night. Her diary entry (p. 245) shows a side to her other than her usual 'dryness': an admission of 'spiteful things' possibly later for 'his eyes' (that is, Charles's), but also for the higher authority of '*His* eyes' (that is, God's).

Chapter 33 resolves the suspense of the 'horror' that met Charles at the door of the barn. The presence of Sam and Mary compromises Charles's position and there is a tacit understanding between Charles and Sam that 'a shrewd sacrifice had just been made' in Sam's refusal to accept money from Charles for his silence. That Charles has done nothing seriously wrong in modern eyes is placed in the Victorian context that he has transgressed, emphasised by the alliterative 'flagrantly fanned the forbidden fire' (p. 249).

CHECK THE BOOK

Susana Onega puts Charles at this point of temptation into a broader context: 'The Gothic literature of the eighteenth and nineteenth centuries was primarily a fictionalisation of the revolt and rebellion of passion against virtue. It is in this context that we should interpret Charles's foreboding that he is entering forbidden and dangerous territory' (Form and Meaning in the *Novels of John Fowles*, 1989, p. 85).

QUESTION

How does the encounter with Sam and Mary pose a threat for Charles? Consider particularly Sam's previous thoughts, his present situation and his refusal of the money from Charles.

Sarah's ability to see through people is evident as she reads Charles's anxieties about the possibility of her committing suicide. The image of the 'lance' with all its connotations returns (p. 251). The phrase 'seeing him whole' is a possible foreshadowing of the wholeness, the Jungian 'individuation', that Charles seeks. The final moment sees Charles deciding between two paths, both literal and metaphorical: the 'field path', or 'the lane that led down to the town' and a meeting with Ernestina.

The meeting between Charles and Ernestina in Chapter 34 contrasts the two women in Charles's life. The description of Ernestina on page 253 is couched in primness and fragility. A cluster of phrases, from the 'rose-pink dress' to the 'froth of gauze' and the 'delicately pervasive fragrance of lavender-water' are summed up in the concluding image of 'a sugar Aphrodite'.

Charles's intention to go to London displeases Ernestina. Their strained relationship is shown in both language and body language. Charles thinks that he will get out of the engagement because of his change in circumstances, though these expectations, like the earlier ones regarding inheritance, will be shown to be misguided. The formal, passionless, almost patronising embrace (a kiss on both temples) becomes, on Ernestina's insistence, a kiss on the lips, which leaves Charles feeling sullied. The final kiss 'hastily on the crown of her head' takes us back to Victorian formality. The chapter ends with a cryptic question: 'What can an innocent country virgin know of sin?' (p. 257).

? QUESTION

What is the general effect of ending a chapter with a question, and what is the specific effect here in Chapter 34?

GLOSSARY	
239	**Paisley** a woollen material with a pattern that incorporates an ornamental cone shape
240	**motes** small particles of dust
	Hegel Georg Wilhelm Hegel (1770–1831), German philosopher
241	**Axminster** a small market town near Lyme Regis
242	**Catullus** Caius Valerius Catullus (c. 84–c. 54 BC), Roman lyrical poet
	Sappho (born c. 650 BC), Greek lyrical female poet, whose love ode was translated into Latin by Catullus

243	lachrymatory causing tears to flow
244	chatelaine female keeper of a castle or large house
245	Janus-like two-faced, contradictory; after Janus, the Roman god of gates, depicted with two heads looking in opposite directions
251	half-hunter a type of watch in a case with a glass window
253	Aphrodite Greek goddess of love
255	Mrs Bloomer Amelia Jenks Bloomer (1818–94), American advocate for women's rights and the woman who introduced 'bloomers', loose-fitting trousers

CHAPTER 35

- Victorian society is condemned for its double standards concerning morality.
- The narrator expresses his views on the hypocrisy that guided Charles's actions.
- Fowles digresses to talk of Thomas Hardy's work and life.

This chapter is a series of digressions from the narrative, though the Victorian issues discussed are applied first to Charles's words and conduct, then to Sam and Mary.

The ambivalence of the Victorian age is portrayed in the juxtaposition of prostitution and religion. The narrator comments on the widespread nature of prostitution in the age, alongside the building of more churches than at any other time in the country's history. A further anomaly is shown in conflicting attitudes to nudity in reality and in art. There was suppression of sexual matters in society and in literature, but a growing output of pornography.

The narrator compares Victorian attitudes to sex with those of the modern age. He then considers the possibility that the puritanical image of the Victorian age may devolve from twentieth-century misconceptions (pp. 260–1). The 'suppression, repression and

 CHECK THE BOOK
The well-received biography of Thomas Hardy by Claire Tomalin is recommended for those wishing to read a thoughtful and sensitive account of Hardy's life (*Thomas Hardy: The Time-Torn Man*, 2006).

CHECK THE BOOK

Lois Deacon and Terry Coleman (*Providence and Mr Hardy*, 1966) propound the argument that the love affair between Hardy and Tryphena Sparks was incestuous – that she was not his cousin, but the illegitimate child of Hardy's own illegitimate half-sister. Eileen Warburton, in her biography of Fowles, suggests that modern scholarship has disproved this theory, though she adds that Fowles did cling to the tenuous legend and its influence as a shaping force behind all of Hardy's fiction.

'silence' of the Victorians may be a distortion of reality based on information provided by the educated middle classes. Sex, marriage and births out of wedlock among the lower classes reveal a much more open attitude to such matters.

This leads into consideration of Thomas Hardy and the stories surrounding an affair with his cousin, Tryphena Sparks. There is a brief examination of the 'facts' of this affair and its effect on Hardy's portrayal of his heroines Sue Bridehead in *Jude the Obscure* and Tess Durbeyfield in *Tess of the d'Urbervilles*.

COMMENTARY

Once again, it is difficult to separate content from commentary, as much of this chapter comprises two lengthy asides: one on the paradoxes in Victorian society (pp. 258–62), and the other on the mysteries surrounding Thomas Hardy's early life (pp. 262–4).

Hardy's proximity to Fowles the novelist can be seen from several perspectives – geographical and literary, as well as in their attitudes to nature, to women, to religion and to social injustice. There are many echoes of Hardy in the **narrative**, besides the more obvious direct **allusions** and the epigraphs.

Ambiguous and, at times, hypocritical Victorian attitudes are placed alongside Charles's ambivalent attitudes towards Sarah. The open minds of the lower classes regarding sexual matters places the affair between Sam and Mary into context, but also comments on the relationship between Charles and Sarah. The narrator considers that the tensions 'between lust and renunciation, undying recollection and undying repression, lyrical surrender and tragic duty, between the sordid facts and their noble use' (p. 264) define not only Hardy, but also the Victorian age. The reader is invited to apply this idea to the various relationships in the narrative.

GLOSSARY	
258	**Marquis de Sade** title of Donatien Alphonse François (1740–1814), French soldier and writer, who wrote about and took part in sexual practices that involved inflicting pain; 'sadism' and 'sadist' derive from his name

259	Dr Bowdler Thomas Bowdler (1754–1825), a writer who rewrote Shakespeare, omitting any risqué elements
260	Naughty Nineties the 1890s, noted for high living and frivolous behaviour
261	Mayhew Henry Mayhew (1812–87), Victorian journalist, author of the book *London Labour and the London Poor* (1851)
	bowdlerized treated in the manner of Dr Bowdler (see above)
262	Pandora's box in Greek mythology, Pandora was the first woman; she opened a box that held all the evils of the world, and thereby released them into the world
	Tolpuddle martyrs in 1834 six labourers from the village of Tolpuddle in Dorset tried to form a trade union and because of this were sentenced to transportation for seven years
263	Edmund Gosse (1845–1928) English poet and critic
	Atreids bronze statues of the sons of Atreus
	Mycenae ancient Greek city where Atreus had his palace
	Egdon Heath setting used in Hardy's *The Return of the Native*, based on heaths near Dorchester

 CHECK THE BOOK

References are made here to several of Hardy's poems: 'At the Wicket Gate', 'She did not turn', 'Her Immortality' (p. 263); also the lines quoted on page 264 from 'The Photograph', in which Hardy regrets burning a photograph of Tryphena. The first epigraph in the novel is from 'The Riddle'. All can be found in *Thomas Hardy: The Complete Poems*, ed. James Gibson, 2001.

CHAPTER 36

- Sarah has taken up residence at the Endicott Family Hotel in Exeter.
- She has made a number of significant purchases.

Sarah has taken two sparsely furnished rooms in a cheap hotel in Exter. She makes purchases that include a roll of bandage, a nightgown and a green shawl. She makes tea and eats, rather inelegantly, a meat pie.

COMMENTARY

This significance of this short chapter will be revealed in Chapter 46, when Charles goes to Sarah's rooms in the hotel. The

CHECK THE BOOK

Linda Hutcheon says, 'Like the narrator, Sarah too pretends not to know things she has really plotted very carefully,' and sums up by adding, 'She is a fine impresario for her own show' ('The "Real World(s)" of Fiction: *The French Lieutenant's Woman*', pp. 128–9).

description of Exeter encapsulates the Victorian anomalies of religion and prostitution, male domination and female inequality. The passage of time is portrayed in the shabbiness of the rooms and their furnishings. The reference is to a Toby jug now in the possession of the twentieth-century narrator (p. 268) is another deliberate **anachronistic** breaking of the Victorian **narrative**.

Among Sarah's purchases is a green shawl, which she holds to her cheek. The movement of the brown-auburn hair on the green shawl, the twisting of the dark green Paisley scarf that she had worn in Carslake's barn (p. 239) and the looking into the mirror add to the sensuality of the moment. The incident here is reminiscent of Mary trying on the green dress earlier (pp. 109–10).

There is a sense of expectancy in the room ('she seemed to be waiting in the quiet light and crackle, the firethrown shadows'), though the narrator will not permit us to enter into her mind (p. 270). Sarah's preparations are precise, as if she is setting the scene for her eventual meeting with Charles. The final detail of the meat pie eaten 'without any delicacy whatsoever' adds a touch of coarseness to Sarah's character. However, the reader must wait until Chapter 46 before the tension is resolved.

GLOSSARY

265	**carbolic** a strong disinfectant cleaning agent
	gin-palaces gaudy drinking houses
266	**murrey** mulberry-coloured, a dark purple
267	**Charles Wesley** (1707–88) English evangelical preacher and writer of hymns
	cornucopias horns overflowing with flowers or fruit
268	**Ralph Wood** (1715–72) designer and maker of Toby jugs – drinking mugs in the shape of a man, or more usually a man's head, wearing a three-cornered hat; a Toby was a market official
269	**merino** long fine wool from the sheep of the same name
	sovereigns gold coins in circulation from 1817 to 1914 and worth one pound sterling

CHAPTERS 37–8

- Charles goes to see Ernestina's father.
- Mr Freeman says that the marriage will go ahead and offers Charles a position in the firm.
- In the London streets Charles finds himself outside Freeman's department store.
- Charles feels trapped and decides to go to his club to drink.

Charles goes to London to meet Ernestina's father. They discuss Charles's change of circumstances and his financial position. While Mr Freeman reads Ernestina's letter, Charles sees a courting couple in the street below. Mr Freeman agrees that the marriage shall proceed. He suggests that Charles join the business as a partner with a view to eventually taking over. Charles is overwhelmed and feels trapped.

He leaves the Freeman house and aimlessly walks the streets, still shocked by what has happened. He senses that the 'lower orders' of society are happier. Charles's discontent stems from the fact that he is now a mere puppet in Freeman's empire. By chance he finds himself outside the Freeman store and the feeling of being trapped increases. He sees himself as a 'drone' (p. 285) and decides that he can never enter commerce. He decides to seek solace in drink.

COMMENTARY

Mr Freeman has ambitions to be a gentleman, his 'determination' possibly covering over 'inner doubt'. Socially he is beneath Charles, but money is an increasing factor in the rise of the middle classes. Freeman's new mansion in Surrey contrasts with Charles's recent loss of Winsyatt. The **ambiguity** of Freeman's position is contrasted by the juxtaposition of his earnest Christianity with the living and working conditions of his employees (p. 272). The **irony** is that, by 1867 standards, Freeman is seen to be advanced in his treatment of workers.

 CHECK THE BOOK

The details of Charles's engagement to Ernestina reflect the traditional concerns of money and class in arranged marriage in nineteenth-century England. In Angus Wilson's novel *No Laughing Matter*, which also appeared in 1967, the class distinction between the parents of the Matthews family is **parodied** in their children's song, 'I brought the breeding and you brought the dough.'

 CHECK THE BOOK

In the years between 1850 and 1875, Britain became, according to E. Royston Pike, 'the world's workshop, the world's carrier, the world's clearing house, the world's banker and a good deal else'. *Human Documents of the Victorian Golden Age 1850–1875* (1967) is a book that Fowles himself commends.

Freeman assesses the financial aspects of the marriage (pp. 275–8) – thinking as the businessman first, though it is shown that eventually 'the gentleman had won'. From this latter perspective, he **ironically** imputes noble motives to Charles. While Freeman reads Ernestina's letter, Charles becomes lost in a Hardyesque cameo scene taking place in the street below – a simple moment in time that contrasts with Charles's own inner conflict about love.

The decision about the marriage made, there is a further contrast in Freeman's control and Charles's helplessness as Freeman broaches the possibility of Charles taking a role in the business and subsequently becoming head of the firm. The offer is first seen by Charles, rather pretentiously, in terms of the temptation of Christ by Satan and the offer of worldly kingdoms. His perception that he is 'a victim of evolution' may be more accurate, but even when he completes Freeman's statement about the need for a species to change and 'adapt itself to changes in the environment' (p. 277) he cannot free himself of his prejudices about class and work. Darwinian analogies with evolution, change and adaptation, seen earlier in the 'cryptic coloration' **allusion** (p. 271), enter into the conversation. Freeman's suggestion that they live in 'an age of progress' is valid, but Charles sees himself instead as 'a victim' of it. In a final, self-important image, he sees himself as 'a lion caged' (p. 278).

CHECK THE BOOK

Peter Wolfe suggests that Freeman's offer of partnership in trade forces Charles to 'test the Darwinian principle that survival depends on adaptation' and concludes, 'his resisting a job reflects an inability to shake free from social class and to change with the times' (Peter Wolfe, *John Fowles: Magus and Moralist*, 1979, p. 142).

As Charles wanders through the London streets, the theme of being trapped in an evolutionary process continues in images of an 'ancient saurian species' and a 'poor living fossil' (p. 281). The horror of trade asserts itself with a shock ('as if by some fatal magic') when Charles emerges from a dark side street and faces the brightly lit Oxford Street store of Mr Freeman (p. 284). The store is seen as some monstrous beast about to devour him and any who came near; the language and menacing effect are similar to those in Zola's description of the coal mine in *Germinal* (Chapter 1).

The delusion of a Victorian gentleman, unwilling or unable to face the reality of the emergent power of commerce, is placed in a broader context, that of 'a man struggling to overcome history'. The struggle is perceived in terms of 'the doctrine of the survival of the fittest' and 'free will' – theories that Charles and Grogan had discussed. However, the chapter ends with Charles's real fear of all that 'Freemanism' represents. If the irony of Freeman's name has not been fully realised, the final paragraphs of Chapter 38 make it clear. Charles's free will leads him not to noble thoughts, capitalised in Victorian style as 'Hope', 'Courage' and 'Determination', but to baser images: 'a bowl of milk punch and a pint of champagne'.

GLOSSARY

271	**Mr Jorrocks** a grocer in the sporting novels of R. S. Surtees (1803–64)
272	**homologue** a being of the same nature
	patina a film or light covering over a surface
	Marcus Aurelius (AD 121–80) Roman emperor
	Lord Palmerston (1784–1865) Anglo-Irish statesman; prime minister 1859–65 and 1885–8
277	**Jesus of Nazareth … Satan** Satan offered Jesus all the kingdoms of the earth if Jesus would bow and worship him (Matthew 4:1–11)
	savoir-vivre knowing how to live (French)
279	**Corinthian** ornate style of classical Greek architecture
280	**setts** cobbled stones
281	**saurian** lizard-like
	fusees long-stemmed matches
	turncocks an official who turns water on and off at the mains
282	**mews** a row of stables converted into housing
	equipages carriages with attendants
284	***nouveau riche*** newly rich (French)
285	**drone** a non-working male honey-bee, whose sole function is to mate with females
	parfit perfect, well-trained (Middle English, from French)
	preux chevaliers brave knights (French)

? QUESTION

What are the effects on Charles of Mr Freeman's offer? Look at Charles's immediate reactions and his later reactions when he is in the London streets. Think in terms of class, being a gentleman, freedom, escape, adaptation, survival.

CHAPTERS 39–41

- Charles visits his club and meets two friends.
- They drink heavily and then go to another club that offers entertainment and prostitutes.
- Charles leaves, but in the street picks up a prostitute who takes him to her rooms.
- Charles, feeling nauseaus after the heavy drinking, is physically sick when he learns that the girl's name is Sarah. She comforts him.
- In an interruption in the action Charles argues with Sam. We then learn how the night ended.

At his London club, Charles meets two friends from university days. The three men consume copious amounts of alcohol and go on to the Terpsichore club, where the entertainment comprises lurid live tableaux of women, even young girls, who may be available for hire after the final performance. There is an aside on prostitution before and after the Victorian era. The narrator inserts an extract from an eighteenth-century book he has found in a bookshop. The extract gives an account of sexual performances in a garish club for gentlemen.

Charles is both revolted and excited by the scenes in 'Ma Terpsichore's'. He leaves suddenly and hails a cab. In the street, he picks up a young prostitute.

The girl takes Charles to her rooms in a narrow side street. Charles hears the sound of a child in the adjoining room. The girl explains that it is her daughter by a soldier who has left her. Charles drinks the cheap wine the girl had sent out for. His desire diminishes, but the girl, naked beneath her peignoir, sits on his knee and encourages him to engage in preliminaries to sex. Charles begins to remove his clothes but is feeling increasingly nauseous and dizzy. He asks the girl her name. As she pulls him down towards her, she reveals that her name is Sarah. At this point the nausea overcomes him and he vomits into her pillow.

QUESTION

On page 301 the narrator suggests that 'intimacy was largely governed by the iron laws of convention'. How does Charles's encounter with the prostitute contrast with this idea?

Chapter 41 is a flash forward in time, as Charles returns home, feeling the effects of the evening. Sam has waited up for him and there is a bitter argument. Charles throws various objects at Sam. Sam tells the housekeeper of this quarrel and hints that there could be other revelations. Charles wakes up the next morning and recalls the events of the previous night in the prostitute's room. The young girl had been caring and went to hail a cab for Charles. While he waited, the child woke up. Charles comforted her by letting her play with his watch. He felt sympathy for the young prostitute and left five sovereigns.

COMMENTARY

The epigraph to Chapter 39 sets the tone for the next three chapters. Charles easily falls into the chauvinistic, patronising attitudes of his former colleagues at Cambridge. The garish aspects of Victorian London are portrayed in the streets (pp. 291–2) before we enter the Terpsichore club. Victorian prostitution and pornography are put into a broader perspective by the insertion of a text found in a second-hand bookshop, an **intertextual** device that permits the narrator to show that sexual exploitation is not confined to the nineteenth century (pp. 293–5). The ambivalence of Charles's attitude, both revolted and sexually excited, is specific to his situation as well as general to Victorian male attitudes. The grotesque nature of prostitution is seen in the despair of the performers, and yet more poignantly in the sad image of 'a child who could only just have reached puberty'.

CONTEXT

Fowles was an avid collector of books and journals. In her biography, Eileen Warburton records his visits to Norman's bookshop in Hampstead, where many of the texts that influenced his own writing were found (Warburton, *John Fowles*, pp. 192–4).

The incidents in the young woman's rooms are significantly more natural than the contrived scenes in the club. The pathos is accentuated by the young woman's circumstances, the child she cares for, her honesty about her life juxtaposed with the slight dishonesty about her charges, and finally by Charles's sympathetic reactions to the child. The watch **motif** (p. 308) will recur (pp. 437 and 441), in literary and realistic coincidences as well as in the context of thematic references to time.

The purpose of the flash forward (pp. 305–6) is to remind us of the influence that Sam might now have over his master. The action after Charles's vomiting shows the humanity of the young woman, who

CHECK THE BOOK

Fowles writes: 'The great nightmare of the respectable Victorian mind was the only too real one created by the geologist Lyell and the biologist Darwin. Until then man had lived like a child in a small room. They gave him – and never was a present less welcome – infinite space and time' ('Notes on an Unfinished Novel', in *Wormholes*, p. 17).

takes care of him, and then Charles's own humanity, when he plays with the child and is generous to the mother.

In incongruous surroundings Charles comes to an understanding in a moment of epiphany. He sees time not as a road but as a room, and sees the 'ultimate hell' as 'infinite and empty space' (p. 309). Charles moves forward in self-understanding, 'suddenly able to face his future, which was only a form of that terrible emptiness'.

However, the abrupt, monosyllabic ending of the chapter ('Then he tapped with his stick') returns us to brusque reality and the less likeable side of Charles's character, which may have been perceived in the **ironic** comment 'no shock to the poor like unearned money'. Charles's privileged position with his own unearned money contrasts sharply with that of the young prostitute.

GLOSSARY

289	**Mytton** John Mytton (1796–1834), English eccentric, sportsman and gambler, a specialist in dangerous physical feats
	Casanova Giovanni Girolamo Casanova de Seingalt (1725–98), an Italian adventurer, famous for sexual escapades
291	*metonymia* the substitution of one word for another associated with it
	puella girl (Latin), but also used to represent a loose woman
292	**lorgnette** spectacles with a handle
	shagreen a type of leather
	viragos man-like women, amazons
	Terpsichore the muse of dancing
	Carmina Priapea XLIV the songs of Priapus (Latin), a collection of erotic poems
293	**Camargo** Marie Camargo (1710–70), a French ballerina who introduced calf-length ballet skirts and became a setter of fashion
	Heliogabalus Roman emperor (AD 218–22); his adopted name is that of the Syrian sun god
	Agamemnon Greek general who commanded the army against Troy in an attempt to recover his wife Helen

	Cleland John Cleland (1709–89), English novelist, publisher in 1750 of *Fanny Hill: Memoirs of a Woman of Pleasure*
	Covey of Town Partridges a group of town prostitutes
	Priapus an ancient god of male sexuality
294	**Crotchet** a perverse notion
	Bumper a cup or glass filled to the brim
295	**Gravesend Wherry** a barge from the River Thames port
296	***danseuse*** female dancer (French)
298	**reticule** a small handbag
299	**cutty** a short clay pipe
300	**moreen** a strong woollen or cotton fabric
303	**Etty** William Etty (1787–1849), English painter, noted for his voluptuous female nudes
303	**Pygmalion** a mythological king of Cyprus, who fell in love with a statue he had carved, which came to life as Galatea
308	**commode** a chair containing a chamber pot beneath the seat
307	**truckle bed** a low bed on wheels
308	**lall** babble, make childish sounds
	brougham a type of horse-drawn carriage
309	**Sartrean experience** discomfort with the human condition; in Sartre's *Huis Clos* (in English, *In Camera*), Hell is an enclosed room with no escape

CHAPTER 42

- Charles receives two letters: one a reply to his letter to Dr Grogan, the other containing only an address.

- Grogan advises Charles that Sarah may follow him to London.

- Sam declares his serious interest in Mary and hints at getting money from Charles to set up a draper's shop.

- Charles refuses to provide the money.

- Later, when he realises that Sam may think of blackmail, Charles says he will consider the matter.

CONTEXT

Letters are often used in Victorian fiction to reveal aspects of character, but also as a means of turning the action of the plot. Here we have three letters and two telegrams to consider in terms of character and plot.

The next morning (Chapter 42) when Charles awakes, Sam brings him two letters. The first is a reply to the letter Charles had sent to Dr Grogan, hiding the facts of his last meeting with Sarah. Grogan warns Charles that Sarah may follow him to London. The second letter contains only an address.

Charles tells Sam that they are to return to Lyme. Sam reveals that he intends to propose to Mary. He hints that he needs money to enable him to secure his future by setting up a drapery business. Charles says that financial help from him is out of the question, but that he will increase Sam's wages to those of a married man. Charles reveals his own change of fortune, though Sam already knows about it.

Charles sends two telegrams: one to the White Lion, the other to Ernestina telling her of his return to Lyme. Sam reads the telegrams. It now emerges that he had steamed open the second letter containing the address. He realises that it is from Sarah and resolves to watch her and Charles.

COMMENTARY

Letters play a significant part in this chapter. The first, Charles's letter to Dr Grogan (p. 311) sent on his return from the meeting with Sarah in Carslake's barn, deliberately conceals the meeting with Sarah in Chapter 33. The language of this letter is formal, and a contrast to events that have taken place in Lyme and London since Charles's last communication with the doctor. Charles's dismissal of these events as 'various other circumstances' is a massive understatement. The reply from Grogan (pp. 311–12) is the voice of Victorian common sense, and is **ironic** in the sense that both the advice and the warning have gone unheeded.

CHECK THE BOOK

'Until Charles's irremediable attachment to this *femme fatale*, Sam's destiny is linked to his master's (much like his namesake, Dickens's Sam Weller)' (Olshen, *John Fowles*, p. 79).

The beginnings of Sam's desertion are found in this chapter as Charles makes another 'fatal mistake' in interpreting Sam's aspirations and intentions (p. 316). Sam's reading of the telegrams and his earlier steaming open of the letter containing the address make him realise that his own future lies in Charles's marriage into the Freeman family. The hint of blackmail is present in the idea that 'the more guilt Charles had the surer touch he became', though the ellipsis after 'but if it went too far …' suggests the doubts that are in Sam's mind about the lengths that he may be prepared to go to in the matter.

? QUESTION

How is the master–servant relationship portrayed in the **narrative**?

GLOSSARY

310	rake a dissolute character
311	*éclaircissement* enlightenment (French)
312	*sub tegmine fagi* under the shade of a beech tree (Latin), first line of the first Eclogue by Virgil
	à la lettre to the letter, literally (French)
	Absolvitur let he/she be absolved (Latin)
314	*penchant* liking (French)
316	*ante* Stanislavski before the realist, improvised dramatic interpretations of Stanislavski, stage name of Konstantin Sergeyevich Alexeyev (1865–1938)
	Uriah Heep a scheming, unpleasant clerk in *David Copperfield* (1849–50), by Charles Dickens
317	escritoire writing desk (French)

CHAPTERS 43–4

- Charles takes the train to Exeter.
- He decides to forget Sarah and marry Ernestina.
- Charles returns to Ernestina, makes a sort of confession and is forgiven.
- There is a traditional, neatly rounded-off ending for Charles and Ernestina.
- The other characters' lives are briefly summed up. Mrs Poulteney's end is humorously appropriate.

In the train to Exeter Charles decides that he must never see Sarah again. Her note with only an address shows no indication of guilt on her part nor any further request of him for the future. He decides to confess to Ernestina. He tells Sam that they will not stay in Exeter, but will take a carriage on to Lyme.

CHECK THE BOOK

Susana Onega comments on the 'first' ending: 'Before he knew Sarah, marriage to Ernestina seemed the only possible course of action, although it inevitably entailed his transformation into a businessman' (*Form and Meaning in the Novels of John Fowles*, p. 87).

QUESTION

What other events in the novel so far seem to have depended on a single, apparently insignificant moment?

CHECK THE BOOK

Peter Conradi suggests: 'The first mutant ending is Charles's sentimental daydream, in which he marries Ernestina, forgets Sarah, gets a taste for business and, surrendering to history, prospers' (*John Fowles*, p. 65).

Chapter 44 sees Charles back in Lyme, where at Mrs Tranter's he shows affection for Ernestina and gives her a brooch. He then begins a confession of sorts about his involvement with Sarah. There is a neat tying up of all the loose ends of the story. Charles and Ernestina are married and have children. Charles's uncle, Sir Robert, produces twins as heirs to Winsyatt. Charles joins the Freeman business, which we are told still flourishes in the present time. The lives of Sam and Mary are summarily dismissed as almost irrelevant. Dr Grogan and Mrs Tranter live to a ripe old age. Mrs Poulteney is appropriately dismissed from salvation.

COMMENTARY

The tone in Charles's thoughts is ambivalent, concern hardly hiding the patronising and distanced 'solicitude for the unfortunate woman's welfare'. Charles's dismissal of recent events is seen **ironically** as his 'awakening' (p. 320).

The pivotal moment is Sam's question, 'Are we stayin' the night, Mr Charles?' (p. 320). The answer given here leads to one **dénouement** of the plot, though, as we will see, the question will be asked again (p. 328). That 'one simple question, one answer to a trivial question, should determine so much' is, in retrospect, a **ludic subversion** of the plotting of **narrative**. The consequences of Charles's answer are seen as stifling ('sucked slowly' through the countryside to his fate 'as if down some monstrous pipe') or deathly (his carriage rolling on as 'mournfully as a tumbril'). Even the weather matches the mood, with cloud and drizzle. Sam, however, sees 'gold on the wet road to Lyme', with Charles's marriage to Ernestina and his own financial security in prospect.

Charles is seen in a self-dramatising role, as 'one of life's victims'. The idea is expressed in appropriately palaeontological terms: 'an ammonite in the vast movements of time' and 'a potential turned into a fossil' (p. 321). This image, however, is close to the real dilemma that Charles must face, if he is to escape his age.

Chapter 44 marks the beginning of the first and false ending of the novel. The sentimental scene of confession and forgiveness is given in the obfuscatory language of Charles as the polite, complacent and patronising Victorian (pp. 323–4). His reference to Sarah by the 'more vulgar application' of her name, and the falsity of the phrase 'one of my little pursuits of the elusive echinoderm' capture his tone and his shallowness. The ellipsis leaves the reader to complete Charles's deceitful tale.

The neat 'And so the story ends' is the narrator's own deceit. The **parody** of the neat Victorian conclusion is sewn up in fifteen lines (p. 325), though the observant reader will notice the ironic 'not' at the start of this fairy-tale ending. Mrs Poulteney is accorded more than double the space as the narrator takes delight in her dismissal from the heavenly gates. Her arrogance, presumption and pomposity, her mistaking St Peter for a butler, are all described with relish. Her final fall into an existentially 'devouring space' is mock-heroically Miltonic, though her 'flouncing and bannering and ballooning' and the image of 'a shot crow' continue the amusement. Her sense of social injustice ('Lady Cotton is behind this') undercuts the true justice of her being sent 'down to where her real master waited' (p. 326).

QUESTION

Deceit plays an important part in the novel. It is seen here in Charles's deceit by omission. What other examples can you find?

GLOSSARY

321	**tumbril** an open cart used to transport sentenced people to execution
325	**Jubilate** opening word of a psalm, meaning 'rejoice' (Latin)

CHAPTERS 45–7

- The narrator admits that the ending just given was only a possibility, and not what really happened.
- The action returns to Sam's question about whether or not they were staying in Exeter.
- They stay, and Charles goes to the Endicott Hotel. He is followed by Sam.
- In Sarah's room Charles has brief sexual intercourse with her.

QUESTION

In the traditional, neatly packaged Victorian ending to the story, we read, 'Sam and Mary – but who can be bothered with the biography of servants? They married, and bred, and died, in the monotonous fashion of their kind' (p. 325). How do you read this? Think in terms of the Victorian age, class, evolution, narrative voice.

? QUESTION

What is the effect of returning to Sam's question about staying the night in Exeter? Consider this question from the points of view of Charles and of Sam.

- He says he will marry Sarah, but then realises that she has deceived him.
- Sarah rejects Charles and he leaves bitterly, without a word.

The narrator, having neatly ended the story, opens Chapter 45 with an admission that this ending was a deception. Charles had imagined it. We are taken back to Sam's enquiry about staying the night in Exeter. Charles decides to stay at the Ship and tells Sam to prepare the rooms. Meanwhile, Charles heads for Endicott's Family Hotel. Sam knows where he is going, quickly leaves the baggage at the Ship and goes to watch Charles's arrival at Endicott's.

In Chapter 46, Charles arrives at the hotel and is told Sarah has a sprained ankle. He goes up to her room, where he finds her wearing a nightgown, with a shawl around her shoulders and her feet on a stool by the fireside. She weeps, but Charles tries to avoid eye contact with her. Fire coals tumble out onto the blanket that covers Sarah's legs and feet.

Charles damps out the sparks. As Sarah moves to replace the blanket, their hands touch. Charles looks at Sarah and embraces her. He carries her to the bedroom, and in passionate haste intercourse takes place. There is silence.

Charles is immediately stricken by guilt, as though Ernestina and her father were accusing him. However, he resolves that he will leave Ernestina and marry Sarah. She says that she cannot marry her, though she does say that she loves him. Charles prepares to leave and says he will decide what to do in the next couple of days. As he is dressing, he notices spots of blood on his shirt and realises that Sarah was a virgin. Her story about Varguennes was false. She admits her deception. Suddenly Charles sees that Sarah is not limping on her supposedly sprained ankle. Sarah refuses to offer any explanation for her conduct. She repeats that Charles cannot marry her and that she will only think of his happiness should they ever meet again. She asks him to leave, and Charles silently rushes out of the room.

COMMENTARY

In Chapter 45, direct intrusion once again breaks the illusion of the trustworthy narrator. The idea of the storyteller at work and the suggestion of the 'detailed and coherent manner' of the previous, trite ending place both in an **ironic** light. Further undercutting of the false ending lies in the admission that (if we had not already worked it out) Charles would have enjoyed 'a life-span of nearly a century and a quarter' (p. 327). The narrator's invitation for the reader to entertain a suspicion, 'not uncommon in literature, that the writer's breath has given out' (p. 327), is part of the **ludic subversion**, as the narrator dismisses the control of the 'I'.

Charles's desertion of Sarah, blamed on 'the personification of a certain massive indifference in things', brings to mind the blind, unfeeling 'god' in the novels of Thomas Hardy. The existentialist themes of freedom and terror surface at the moment of choice in the 'anxiety of freedom' that Charles senses. The alternative answer to Sam's question leads to a different sequence of events, a metaphorical fork in the **narrative** path and a **parodic** exposure of the illusions of both Victorian and **postmodernist** fictions.

Chapter 46 takes us back to Chapter 36, where Sarah's purchases and preparation of the room seemed innocent enough, though now we reassess her motives. The eating of the meat pie 'without any delicacy whatsoever' (p. 270) takes on a new significance in the light of the orchestration of the scene. The seemingly careful preparations conspire to ensnare Charles in the long-awaited consummation of the relationship. The speed at which this takes place is specific, ninety seconds, but sufficient to alter Charles's future. The rushed syntax of the 'torrent of things banned, romance, adventure, sin, madness, animality' captures the passion of the moment (p. 336).

The single word, 'Silence', that opens Chapter 47 creates a pause before the aftermath is expressed in terms of the twentieth-century horror of the atom bomb, a horror alive in the collective consciousness of the 1960s because of the Cuban missile crisis.

Charles's first reaction is that he has used Sarah to satisfy his lust. However, the blood spots (pp. 340–1) and the normal walking on

 QUESTION

What connections do you note between the events of Chapter 36 (pp. 267–70) and those of Chapter 46 (pp. 332–7)? Look closely at the details in each episode.

CHECK THE BOOK

'Charles discovers that, despite having played the role of fallen woman, Sarah was in fact a virgin. She thus combines both halves of the Victorian typology: at exactly the point she ceases to be a virgin she begins for the first time *to appear to have been one*' (Peter Conradi, *John Fowles*, 1982, p. 65).

the ankle reveal that he has been deceived, which sets in motion a recognisably Victorian reaction. Sensational fiction ('Why? Why? Why? Blackmail! To put him totally in her power!') and the **Gothic** ('those loathsome succubi of the male mind') followed by a litany of horrors (p. 341) are part of the **parody**. Sarah's refusal to explain her motives and her statement 'You cannot marry me, Mr Smithson' drive Charles from the room, and we are left as perplexed as Charles by the mystery.

GLOSSARY		
328	prolix	long and wordy
	Delphic	ambiguous, difficult to interpret; from the oracle at Delpi in ancient Greece
330	browns	copper pennies
341	succubi	devils supposed to invade men's sleep in female form

CHAPTERS 48–9

- Charles wanders through the Exeter streets and sees a church.
- Alone inside the church, he agonises with his conscience.
- He realises that he must choose Sarah in order to find freedom. He decides to break with Ernestina, and sends Sam to Sarah with a letter containing a brooch.
- Sam says there was no answer to the letter, and Charles believes that Sarah has kept the brooch.
- Sam tells Mary all that he knows and makes plans to leave his master.

Charles leaves Endicott's Hotel and walks into a run-down area of the town. He enters a church. The curate is just locking up, but he leaves Charles the key. Alone, Charles sits and stares at the crucifix above the altar. He says the Lord's Prayer and then composes his own prayer for forgiveness. He sees a vision of Sarah on the cross. He weeps. Charles is torn between agnosticism and a need for faith, but he cannot communicate with God. He engages in a dialogue with himself. He approaches the crucifix and is aware of the real essence of Christianity. He sees his failure and the failure of his age. His thoughts go back to a future with Sarah.

In the next chapter Charles returns the key to the curate's house. He now believes he understands Sarah's deceit. He rehearses a scene of reconciliation with her. In the street he meets Sam and returns with him to the Ship. Charles begins to wash the blood stains from his clothes, but leaves them only half done. Sam clears the garments away. Charles writes to Sarah proposing marriage. However, he decides not to send the letter until the next morning in order to make her suffer a little. He considers dismissing Sam.

Next morning Charles sends Sam with the letter, placing inside it the brooch that he gave to Ernestina in the false ending of Chapter 44. Sam returns, and says that there was 'No answer' (p. 358). Charles believes Sarah has received the letter and kept the brooch.

The chapter closes with Sam telling Mary all he knows about Charles and Sarah. He plans to leave Charles and believes that he knows a way of obtaining the money he needs for his future.

COMMENTARY

Ironically, Charles the agnostic ('He knew in that dark church that the wires were down') finds some understanding inside the deserted church. The fact that he must reach this understanding alone is accentuated by the curate leaving him the key and a stranger trying the locked door. In a dialogue between 'his better and his worse self', the better self pulls him back from despair (p. 347). As he moves towards the crucifix over the altar, he senses that Sarah is with him, as if waiting for the marriage service, 'yet with another end in view'.

At this moment an epiphany strikes Charles, in 'a sudden flash of illumination', (p. 349). He sees through the 'barbarous image' on the cross to true Christian understanding: that the answer does not lie in the image, but in a descent from the cross into the real world of 'living men and women'. Charles is here not so much the Victorian

CHECK THE BOOK

John Fawkner argues: 'From a certain point of view she [Sarah] seems bent on crucifying him [Charles]. Her real aim is to uncrucify herself, and in this she becomes much more than an individual desiring personal freedom. She comes to embody the emancipation of woman' (*The Timescapes of John Fowles*, p. 86).

CHECK THE BOOK

Simon Loveday makes the comment: 'In a sense the lonely figure outside the locked church, like a believer lamenting the impossibility of belief, is far more like Charles's creator than like Charles himself' (*The Romances of John Fowles*, p. 79).

QUESTION

What is there in the incident in the church to suggest that Charles is moving forwards towards understanding of the whole self, in spite of elements that hold him back?

man caught in time, but any man facing his age with all 'its iron certainties and rigid conventions'. The feeling that he is not alone but with 'a whole dense congregation of others' strengthens the universality (p. 350). Charles's 'glimpse of another world', however, is placed sharply into context, as we are reminded that this may be 'another chapter from his hypothetical autobiography' (p. 351), in which worldly thoughts of his uncle's marriage and his own to Sarah surface. Charles has the 'belief that Sarah on his arm in the Uffizi' represents freedom. The radiance on his face is not so much a truly spiritual change like that of St Paul, for his back is to the altar and the radiance is bathetically expressed as possibly 'that from the gaslight by the steps'. The incident, however, is one stage in his still incomplete progress towards understanding himself – the Victorian man experiencing existential angst, and rejecting the conventional morality of duty towards Ernestina.

Chapter 49 opens with Charles's decision to break with Ernestina and marry Sarah, though the Victorian chauvinist in him delays sending the letter to Sarah until the next morning so that she will suffer a little (p. 357). The letter proves crucial as it and the brooch that had featured in the false ending are not delivered. Sam's deception and decision to desert are increasing as he sees Ernestina and her fortune slipping away (p. 359).

GLOSSARY

345	**Mater Dolorosa** the grieving mother (Latin); the mother of Jesus after the crucifixion
	Grünewald Matthias Grünewald (c. 1480–1528), German artist whose altarpiece painting in Colmar shows the Mater Dolorosa
	Colmar, Coblenz, Cologne northern German cities, the first of these actually the location of Grünewald's altarpiece
	Bradlaugh Charles Bradlaugh (1833–91), a social reformer
348	**render unto Caesar** an **allusion** to the words of Jesus that distinguished between political and divine authority (Matthew 22:21)
351	**ormolu** gold leaf used to gild bronze

352	**Damascus** on the road to Damascus, Saul was blinded by a light and a heavenly voice asked why he persecuted Christians; on recovering his sight, he accepted the Christian faith and became St Paul
	Uffizi an art gallery in Florence, Italy
353	***en passage*** in transit, passing through (French)
	Tractarian belonging to the Oxford religious movement
355	***Dr Jekyll and Mr Hyde*** novel by Robert Louis Stevenson in which the good Dr Jekyll transforms into the evil Mr Hyde
357	**anabatic** rising upwards

CHAPTERS 50–3

- Charles breaks off his engagement to Ernestina, who threatens him with legal action.
- Charles goes to fetch Dr Grogan to attend to her.
- Sam gives in his notice to Charles.
- Dr Grogan tells Mrs Tranter of Charles's actions in breaking off the engagement; Mrs Tranter says that she will help Sam and Mary.
- Dr Grogan condemns Charles for his actions. He still believes Sarah has duped Charles.

 QUESTION

What does the choice of words used here reveal about Ernestina's immediate attitude to Charles's news and her overall character? Pay particular attention to the intensity of individual words.

Charles returns to Mrs Tranter's house. He tells Ernestina that he is breaking off their engagement. He claims to have met a former lover, but does not reveal that the woman is Sarah. Ernestina is incredulous, but when she sees that Charles is serious her anger increases. She threatens legal action. As Charles is leaving, she calls out and falls down in a faint that seems rather contrived. Charles tells Ernestina that he will write to her father. He goes to fetch Dr Grogan and tells Mary to look after Ernestina until the doctor arrives.

Chapter 50 begins with the conversation between Charles and Grogan. Grogan guesses that Sarah is involved in Charles's decision

CHECK THE BOOK

Thomas C. Foster says that 'Marriage to her [Ernestina] would mean ossification for Charles: his tendencies toward stiffness, toward propriety, toward conventionality, would overcome his countervailing impulses toward flexibility, independent thought, and individual action' (*Understanding John Fowles*, p. 78).

CONTEXT

Dante Alighieri (1265–1321) was an Italian poet and author of *The Divine Comedy*. In 'The Inferno' section of *The Divine Comedy*, Dante describes the punishment in Hell of the Antinomians (p. 378), a sect that believed that faith is sufficient for salvation and that moral law is not necessarily binding, freeing their choice of action.

to end the engagement. Charles returns to the White Lion, where Sam tells hims that he will leave his employment. They part angrily. Charles looks back over his actions, and almost considers trying to reverse what he has done. However, thoughts of Sarah push such ideas out of his mind. As he is writing to Mr Freeman, Grogan arrives.

Chapter 52 takes us back to Mrs Tranter's house. On her return, she finds the house in confusion. Dr Grogan has given Ernestina a sedative. He tells Mrs Tranter what has happened and suggests that he will talk to Charles. Mary tells Mrs Tranter of her love for Sam. She reveals that Sam has left Charles's employment. Mrs Tranter says that she will find a post for Sam and that Mary will stay with her until she is married.

In Chapter 53 Grogan asks Charles to explain his actions. Grogan condemns Charles for his treatment of Ernestina and again expresses doubts about Sarah. He offers Charles advice about the 'elect' and their responsibilities in the world. If they follow selfish desires, they fail the test of morality and become 'no more than despots, sultans, mere seekers after their own pleasure and power' (p. 381). Charles is left to consider Grogan's words.

COMMENTARY

The main interest in these four chapters lies in the progress of the action. Charles's decision to break off the engagement and his decision's effects on Ernestina, Mary, Mrs Tranter and Dr Grogan all follow swiftly in a flurry of action: Ernestina's incredulity, her increasing anger and her somewhat contrived faint (pp. 361–8); Mary's distress; Mrs Tranter's sadness and altruism (pp. 374–7); Grogan's Victorian disapproval (pp. 378–82); and Sam's possible future all figure in the aftermath of Charles's choice. Charles's romanticised thoughts of Sarah show again that he can observe at a superficial level but not fully understand the significance of what he sees.

In Chapter 53 Grogan's conversation with Charles reveals that he, like Charles, is a man of science and learning but trapped in the Victorian age. Amid the general disapproval, Grogan does touch on a significant idea, that of the elect and their responsibility in the world (p. 381). The title of *The Aristos*, Fowles's collection of aphorisms, is variously translated as the 'Few', the 'Excellent', deriving from *aristoi*, the Athenian noblemen of excellent character. In his advice to Charles here, Grogan may be seen in the role of the Jungian older man as guide to the searcher for wholeness of being.

CONTEXT

Speaking to Jan Relf, Fowles asserts that the responsibility of the Few is 'being a little more honest than convention or social circumstances will usually allow' ('An Interview with John Fowles', Harry Ransom Humanities Research Centre, University of Texas, 1985; reprinted in Vipond, ed., *Conversations with John Fowles*, p. 122).

GLOSSARY

363	**Helen of Troy** in Greek mythology, the beautiful woman whose elopement with Paris brought about the fall of the city of Troy
	Cleopatra queen of Egypt, famed for her charm and beauty
366	**vitriol** literally sulphuric acid, metaphorically caustic criticism
368	**catatonia** a type of schizophrenia causing rigidity or immobility
371	**Judas** Judas Iscariot was the disciple who betrayed Jesus
	Ephialtes a Greek traitor who betrayed his fellow Athenians by showing the enemy a secret path behind their lines
372	**bantam** a cockerel, hence a small and aggressive man or soldier
375	***non sequitur*** a statement that does not follow logically from what has been previously said
	linnet a small bird
	stocks a place of public punishment, a frame in which a criminal was locked
379	**commination** denunciation, a recital of divine judgement against sinners
380	**excommunication** formal expulsion from a religious group
381	**elect** chosen few, usually in spiritual terms, i.e. those chosen by God
	Jacta alea est the die is cast (Latin); the words attributed to Julius Caesar once he had crossed the Rubicon river into Gaul, meaning that there was no turning back

CHAPTERS 54–6

- Charles goes to Exeter, where he finds that Sarah has left and that Sam has deceived him.
- On the train to London the narrator enters Charles's compartment and studies him.
- The narrator discusses his problems of concluding the narrative. He will offer two endings, and he tosses a coin to decide which will come first.
- Charles has to sign a legal document for his breach of promise.
- Charles fails in his search to find Sarah and finally decides to travel abroad.

QUESTION

How do you react to the appearance of the narrator as a character in the narrative? You could consider Chapter 13, other intrusions by the narrator, and any critiques you have read.

Charles goes to Sarah's hotel, only to find that she has gone to London, leaving no address. He discovers that his letter and the brooch were never delivered to Sarah and that Sam has deceived him.

Chapter 55 opens as Charles takes the train to London. With cold looks, he deters passengers from entering his compartment. However, a bearded stranger enters and sits down. As Charles sleeps, the stranger begins to examine him closely. The stranger now reveals his identity as the narrator of the story. He is confused about what to do with Charles and how to end his story. Moreover, he admits that he does not know where Sarah is. He realises that two endings are possible. He then decides that he will offer both endings and tosses a coin to see which will come first so as not to influence the reader's interpretation of the outcome. As the train enters the London station, the two men go their separate ways.

www. **CHECK THE NET**

Visit **www. victorianlondon. org** for links to the 'breach of promise' reference – click on 'Women' and then 'Courtship, Marriage & Romance'.

In Chapter 56 Charles begins his search for Sara, employing private detectives. In the midst of this, Charles receives a summons from Mr Freeman's solicitors. Charles attends the meeting, accompanied by his own solicitor, Mr Montague. There will be no court case but Charles must sign a legal document admitting breach of promise. It will permit Mr Freeman to use this admission should Charles ever decide to marry. Charles feels humiliated and wishes to leave England. He continues to search in vain for Sarah. After another week, he abruptly decides to go abroad.

COMMENTARY

Charles's initial confidence in the fulfilment of his future with Sarah is expressed in the optimism that develops in the first section of Chapter 54 (pp. 383–4). The natural images are hopeful ('rich green fields and May hedgerows'). His thoughts are positive ('new life', 'great challenges', even guilt which seems 'beneficial'). The harmony that he and Sarah will share is encapsulated in the image of the pharaoh and his wife, both carved from the same stone. Charles has not yet realised that the Egyptian image Sarah most resembles is the enigmatic Sphinx (see Chapter 60). His illusions are expressed in a flow of Romantic thoughts of travel and exotic images ('moonlight', 'singing gypsies', the scent of jasmine). The exile that Charles sees is a shared exile, but this idea is soon dispelled by Sarah's complete disappearance.

Charles's search for Sarah and the visit to the solicitor's for legal advice bring him into contact with two aspects of Victorian law, the private detective and the legal proceedings overseen by the fearsome Serjeant Murphy with his 'vulpine smile' and 'basilisk quiz' (pp. 394–5). The outcome of the six statements in the legal document accentuates Charles's lonely future, though he continues to search for Sarah. His decision to travel abroad is abrupt, though it may have something to do with an unwilling acceptance of Montague's belief in Dr Grogan's assessment of Sarah's 'motive of vindictive destruction' (p. 399).

CHECK THE POEM

A similar image to the stone sculpture appears in the poem 'An Arundel Tomb', the final poem in Philip Larkin's *The Whitsun Weddings* (1964), which makes some interesting comments about relationships, time and love.

CHECK THE BOOK

For the portrayal of another fearsome legal character, look at the solicitor Jaggers in *Great Expectations* by Charles Dickens.

GLOSSARY

384	**Alhambra** the Moorish palace above the city of Granada in southern Spain
385	**aboulia** loss of will power, inability to make decisions
387	**Gorgon** one of three mythical monsters with the ability to turn all who looked at them to stone
	Spurgeon Charles Spurgeon (1834–92), a popular Baptist preacher

continued

388	douce soft, gentle
	Cullompton town in Devon
391	ubiquity the ability to seem to be everywhere; from *ubique*, everywhere (Latin)
393	*confessio delicti* an admission of guilt (Latin)
	Inns of Court the four legal societies that have the right of calling candidates to the bar
394	ferret silk or cotton ribbon
	columbarium a funeral vault for urns containing ashes of the dead
	vulpine fox-like
395	basilisk a mythical serpent that could kill with a glance or a breath
396	*sine die* without a fixed date (Latin)
398	Verrey's a London restaurant
399	*prima facie* on the face of things, at first sight (Latin)

CHAPTER 57

- The action moves forward twenty months.
- Sam has married Mary and is prospering in family life and in the Freeman business in London.
- Mary recognises Sarah entering a house on the Embankment.
- She tells Sam, who feels guilty about the past.

QUESTION

What factors are significant in the rise of Sam and Mary in the world? You could include thoughts about the Victorian age, change and adaptation.

It is twenty months later. A woman, carrying a child and clearly expecting another, walks along the Thames embankment. She notices a woman alighting from a cab. The expectant woman is revealed as Mary. The other woman, who enters a house, is Sarah.

Mary and Sam are happily married. Sam has joined Mr Freeman's business and done well. His window display brings about Freeman's approval and reward. He still longs for his own business, but Mary realises that security lies with his employment at Freeman's store.

They are rising in the world, and Mary has a servant of her own. She also has the brooch that Sam had taken from Charles's letter to Sarah.

Sam's conscience troubles him after Mary reveals that she has seen Sarah.

COMMENTARY

This chapter acts as a break in time and in the **narrative** between Charles leaving England (p. 399) and his return some twenty months later (p. 419). The intervening time in these chapters deals with the rise of Sam and Mary in the world. Their success in the Freeman enterprise suits Sam's native sharpness and initiative. His success in the same world that Charles rejected is a comment on their different personal responses to change as well as a broader sociological comment about the changes in the order of Victorian society. There is a hard reality about this success in the 'Oxford Street grindstone' (p. 405), though with a skivvy of her own now Mary is determined that Sam should continue in the trade.

The accidental discovery of Sarah's whereabouts is made by Mary (pp. 400–1). The narrator's awareness of approaching spring is complemented by the opening two words of a poem or song by Catullus ('*Iam ver …*'), musing on the approach of warm winds. The narrator draws the reader into participation in the discovery, which is finally revealed in Mary's ''Twas 'er, Sam'. The narrator still playfully inserts deliberate **anachronisms**, this time the perambulator, which did not appear for another decade.

The **motif** of the brooch reappears, 'the emblem of their good fortune', but now, since Sam has a conscience, it is something that must be paid for (p. 406). This takes us back and also forward in time as we anticipate what the price for Sam will be.

CHECK THE BOOK

Jerry White records the rise of the department store in London, noting Whiteley's (1863), which in four years had grown to seventeen departments, Harrod's (1853) expanding rapidly between 1860 and 1879, and several others in the great store-building period after the turn of the century, especially at the Marble Arch end of Oxford Street (*London in the Nineteenth Century*, 2008, p. 191).

CHECK THE POEM

The opening lines of this poem or song by Gaius Valerius Catullus, *Iam ver egelidos refert tepores / iam ceali furor aequinoctalis / iucundis Zephyri silescit auris*, is translated as: 'Now Spring brings back the soothing warmth; the rage of the equinoctial sky is silenced by the sweet winds of Zephyr.'

GLOSSARY

400	Mill's *Subjection of Women* (1869) book advocating votes for women, by John Stuart Mill
	Girton College the first college for women at Cambridge University
404	**good wine needs no bush** real quality does not need to be advertised (the bush was the ancient sign outside an inn)
405	**Faust** in the Faust (or Faustus) legend, Faust sold his soul to the devil Mephistopheles for knowledge and pleasure, and eventually had to pay the price

CHAPTERS 58–9

- Charles travels widely in Europe and the Middle East.
- He finds some solace in poetry.
- Over a year later he returns to London, but then leaves for America.
- Charles meets many women, but Sarah is still in his mind.
- In New Orleans he receives news that Sarah has been found, and he returns to London.

 CHECK THE POEM

Maud by Alfred, Lord Tennyson (appointed Poet Laureate in 1850), is a dramatic monologue that describes the love of a young man for Maud, the daughter of a man who has ruined him. The young man kills Maud's brother in a duel. Maud dies, and the protagonist faces a tragic exile.

Chapter 58 chronicles Charles's travels across Europe. He usually travels alone, reads and writes poetry. His favourite poems are Tennyson's *Maud* and Matthew Arnold's 'To Marguerite'. He travels for fifteen months, never once returning to England.

Before Charles left he had visited his uncle and his new wife. He declined the offer of the Little House. News reaches Charles that his uncle has produced a son, heir to the title and the money. Charles accepts the news without much emotion. He has casual affairs with women, but he remains emotionally detached. He sees Sarah as two different figures in his life: the one a personification of Eve, the other a scheming, half-mad governess.

He meets two Americans from Philadelphia. For a time, he enjoys their company and sees an attraction in the American way of life. Back in London after fifteen months, Charles decides he will go to America.

Chapter 59 begins with a stormy crossing of the Atlantic before Charles lands in Boston. He admires the city and its people. He receives social invitations and visits the sights. Though there is still hostility to the British, Charles is accepted since he does not seem to be typically British. He meets American women, though there is no romance. Charles still thinks of the legal document and its terms. American women remind Charles of Sarah. He travels south and sees the effects of the Civil War and the Reconstruction period. The narrator interrupts the American travels with a paragraph that reveals news of Sam and Mary. A second child, a boy, has been born.

CHECK THE NET
For a history of Boston and a link to the history of the United States, try **www. localhistories.org/ bostonus.html**

Sam tells Montague, Charles's solicitor, where Sarah can be found. Immediately on receipt of the cable in New Orleans, Charles returns to England.

COMMENTARY

The theme of freedom and its corollary, entrapment, runs through Chapter 58. Travel becomes for Charles a form of escapism, and he loses interest in palaeontology and his London house. The omniscient narrator tells us that he 'would never live in it' (p. 407). Poetry is a solace, with Tennyson's *Maud* Charles's favourite along with Matthew Arnold's 'To Marguerite', which he has learnt by heart. The four verses of the poem are reproduced in full in the text (pp. 408–9), and its message and imagery are significant in the narrative, particularly in the final paragraph of the book. *Maud* may attract Charles for its story of lost love and exile, while 'To Marguerite' seems even closer to his existentialist sense of isolation and loss of faith in a hostile world. The extended quotations embellish the narrative and contribute to the Victorian *zeitgeist* (spirit of the age).

CHECK THE NET
For a website that takes you on a Grand Tour experience, visit **www.umich.edu** and enter 'Grand Tour' into the search box.

Charles's touring of Europe mirrors the idea of the Grand Tour, a cultural journey across the art galleries and buildings of major cities, notably in France, Italy, Germany and Holland (pp. 409–11). When Charles mentions a chance encounter with two Americans to Montague, it introduces the possibility in the lawyer's mind that Sarah may have gone to America. Whether this is in Charles's mind, or whether he is attracted to the Philadelphians' criticism of England and the possibility of a country with 'very similar views to his own', is left open to interpretation. There is a small and significant italicisation in Montague's emphasis on the word 'her' (p. 412). We are again left in doubt whether this is out of deference to Charles's feelings or a passing reference to Sarah's sexuality.

Chapter 59 deals with travels across the United States in the period after the Civil War. Charles does not fully understand 'the strange vastness and frustrated energy of this split nation', but he does note how far advanced the feminist movement is and believes that Sarah 'would have been at home here' (p. 415). Thoughts of Sarah are still present in the 'shadow of Sarah' seen in many of the faces of American women. However, Charles reminds himself of the 'dreadful document' that he signed and realises that it is only Sarah, already beyond the pale, who could 'exorcise' those conditions (p. 414).

The portrayal of Charles on a promontory facing the sea and Europe (p. 416) is almost a mirror image of Sarah herself at the start of the book, on the Cobb, facing the sea. It is shortly after this, in New Orleans, that Charles receives the news of Sarah's having been found.

QUESTION

What does Charles learn about America and about himself during his American tour?

GLOSSARY	
407	**dragoman** a guide or an interpreter in Eastern countries
408	**khans** inns (Arabic)
	alberghi inns (Italian)
411	**Leghorn** English name for Livorno, the Italian seaport
	Avignon city in the south of France
	Vézelay an abbey in the south of France
	Canaan the land flowing with milk and honey, the Promised Land for the Israelites in the Bible
412	**Pocahontas** (1595–1617) American Indian girl who saved English colonist John Smith from execution at the hands of her father

412	*pour la dot comme pour la figure* as much for the dowry as for the face (French)
413	**storm-basin** a basin for those suffering from sea-sickness
	Athenaeum an independent library, museum and gallery in Boston
	Bunker Hill the first engagement in the American Civil War in Charleston, now part of Boston
	Lowell circle in Cambridge the Lowells were an influential family in the United States in the city of Cambridge, Massachusetts, the location of Harvard University
	loxodromic following the curve of a sphere, usually related to sailing
414	**Faneuil Hall** a market hall and meeting place in Boston
	Civil War the American war between the Southern Confederate and the Northern Unionist states (1861–5)
	Uncle Sam traditional figure representing the United States
	Anti-Slavery Movement a movement in America to abolish slavery, eventually successful in 1863–5
	Harvard the famous American University
	contretemps argument, dispute
	farded flashy
415	**Common** the open central park area in Boston
	Reconstruction the period after the Civil War, when the American South was reorganised into the union of states
	Andrew Johnson (1808–75) the seventeenth president of the United States
	Ulysses S. Grant (1822–85) the eighteenth president of the United States
416	**chicanery** trickery
	carpet-baggers adventurers from the northern states who sought to create a political career in the South after the Civil War
417	**iambic slog-and-smog** plodding lines of verse
	stogy a cheap cigar

CONTEXT

The 'master' referred to on p. 414 is Henry James (1843–1916), an American novelist who became a British citizen, a transition the exact opposite of Charles's move to the United states. Rye is the town in East Sussex where Henry James settled after his move to England.

CHAPTER 60

- Montague gives Charles details about the finding of Sarah, who is now known as Mrs Roughwood.
- Charles visits the house where Sarah is living. He tells her of his broken engagement and his searches for her.
- She is dressed in the style of the New Woman and is living with the Pre-Raphaelites, working for them as an assistant.
- There is some misunderstanding about the 'other' person in her life, a child, who turns out to be Charles's daughter.
- Sarah and Charles are reconciled, and the story ends with a suggestion of marriage and happiness.

Montague has received Sarah's address, but he is unaware who provided this information. The person sought no reward for the information. Sarah is now known as Mrs Roughwood. Charles goes to the house where she is living. A woman answers the door, reads Charles's calling card and tells the man behind her that Charles wishes to see Sarah. He is shown upstairs. He recognises modern art on display, as well as the monogram on some of the paintings.

Charles is told that Sarah is no longer a governess. As he waits, Charles recognises another gentleman. He is shocked as he realises that Sarah is living with this group of Pre-Raphaelite artists. Sarah appears, dressed in the style of the New Woman. She looks younger, and he associates her with American fashion.

Sarah reveals that she is an assistant to the artist, sometimes serving as a model. Charles knows the reputation of the artist and his friends, one of whom is a notorious poet. He begins to explain what happened, though Sarah says that she knew of his broken engagement. Her name was changed when she saw one of Charles's requests for information. She states that she is not the mistress of the artist. She has found a new affection, but has no desire to marry.

Sarah is happy in her position, feeling that she belongs. She will not listen to Charles's advances, nor to his resentment that she has

 CHECK THE BOOK

Fowles provides an answer to the question of the two endings: 'from early in the first draft I was torn intolerably between wishing to reward the male protagonist (my surrogate) with the woman he loved and wishing to deprive him of her – that is, I wanted to pander to both the adult and the child in myself' ('Hardy and the Hag', in *Wormholes*, p. 145).

CONTEXT

The term 'New Woman' was coined in the nineteenth century to describe the emerging type of woman who challenged conventional gender roles and sought female autonomy and individuality.

destroyed his life. As he leaves, Sarah asks him to meet a 'lady' who understands her and who wishes to see him. Charles does not understand, though he has suspicions and is still angry. He believes it will be the sister of the artist. However, it is the girl who had shown him up to her room. She is holding a child. Charles is left with the child and he realises that it is his daughter. Charles entertains the child with his watch. When Sarah returns, she tells Charles that the girl is called Lalage. There follows a reconciliation, and the chapter closes with the suggestion of marriage and happiness as a family.

COMMENTARY

Montague, having revealed Sarah's address, half-jokingly suggests that Charles must 'question the Sphinx', and warns about the fate of those who failed to solve its riddle (p. 420). The **narrative** is showing further echoes of the beginning of the book. Another such echo is the fact that the house belongs to one of the Pre-Raphaelites. With mock discretion, the narrator demurs about revealing names. Half suggestions and implicit detail invite the reader to play the identification game (pp. 422–3). The clues, however, are strong enough to identify the artist Dante Gabriel Rossetti, his sister Christina, the critic John Ruskin and the poet Algernon Charles Swinburne before the narrator rather disingenuously declares 'I will hide names no more' (p. 435).

Charles's intentions are placed in the rather comical context of medieval Romance. He is metaphorically 'in full armour, ready to slay the dragon'. But the 'damsel had broken all the rules' so that Charles appears foolish (p. 426). Doubts about Sarah's affections and any commitment to Charles run through their conversation. Sarah's revelation that there is 'another' is an additional part of the riddle she poses. Her desire to be independent is expressed directly: she states 'I wish to be what I am' and 'I do not wish to marry'. Her sense of completion is again simple and direct: 'I am at last arrived' (p. 430).

Her revelation that she knew that Charles had not married and that he had sought her through agencies and advertisements is a bitter pill for Charles to swallow. Charles's bitterness is expressed in

CHECK THE NET

For excerpts from *The Pre-Raphaelite Art of the Victorian Novel* by Sophia Andres, a book that traces the connections between the art of the Pre-Raphaelites and the novels of Collins, Eliot, Gaskell and Hardy, visit **www. ohiostatepress. org** and enter 'Andres Pre-Raphaelite' into the search box.

melodramatic language: his life is 'ruined', he is about to receive the '*coup de grâce*', he is 'a new victim', and he says she has 'planted the dagger in my breast'. His final declamation condemns her to a punishment that 'shall outlast eternity' (p. 433).

Sarah persists in the enigma, half-revealing the truth about the 'lady' who knows her and the 'truth that a less honourable gentleman would have guessed some time ago'. The climax comes in the scene with the small child, two years old and clearly meant to be seen as Charles's daughter, however far-fetched it may seem from the ninety-second consummation. The **motif** of the watch takes the reader back to a similar scene with the young prostitute's child. The child's name, Lalage, which Sarah says means 'to babble like a brook', recalls the 'lall' of the prostitute's baby (p. 308). It also goes further back to the babbling of the streams in the Undercliff (p. 71) and picks up the image of Sarah's sorrow seen as flowing like 'water out of a woodland stream' (p. 16).

The action now progresses to a **parody** of the Victorian ending – reconciliation, embraces, and understandings of past events 'in God's hands, in His forgiveness of their sins'. The musical motif, the poor playing of the piano in a distant house by 'an amateur, a lady with time on her hands', follows the moment of the child playing with the watch (p. 437). The idea that the music is the only 'progression' and that history for Charles has become 'a living stop, a photograph in the flesh' fixes the moment in time. Musical imagery brings the chapter to its sentimental conclusion, as the distant piano music stops, replaced by the suggestion of 'a thousand violins' and the 'percussion' of Lalage's doll on Charles's cheek (p. 439). The final understanding is expressed in religious terms: 'the rock of ages can never be anything else but love, here, now'. The reader knows that this is the second of three alternative endings, and so anticipates the final chapter with its different conclusion.

CHECK THE BOOK
Commenting on the ending of the **narrative** in Chapter 60, Mahmoud Salami says, 'The second ending represents Charles's choice of freedom by uniting with Sarah, but Sarah herself refuses to be inscribed, dominated by him. In short, this ending is a kind of wish-fulfillment of Charles's fantasies of a happy life with her' (*John Fowles's Fiction and the Poetics of Postmodernism*, 1992, p. 132).

GLOSSARY

419	**copperplate** a fine handwriting style
420	**Sphinx** a monster in Greek mythology with the head of a woman and the body of a lioness: those who could not answer the riddles it posed were strangled; in a general sense, anone who is seen as enigmatic or inscrutable
421	**cachet** distinctive mark or characteristic
	wisteria a climbing, flowering shrub
422	**sibylline** like a sibyl, an ancient Greek or Roman oracle or prophetess
424	**dianthus** a flower of the same family as the carnation
424	**pupa** an intermediate stage of development, usually of insects
425	*bas relief* a technique in sculpture where the figures stand out only slightly from the base on which they are formed
	amanuensis a secretary, a literary assistant
	amphora a two-handled jar
426	**John Morley** (1838–1923) English journalist, writer, philosophical critic and politician
	ménage à quatre – à cinq a living arrangement involving four or five, the usual phrase being *ménage à trois* for a household of three
428	**Mr Ruskin** John Ruskin (1819–1900), English author and art critic, supporter of the Pre-Raphaelites
429	**Noel Humphreys** Henry Noel Humphreys (1810–79), English artist, noted for designs and illustrated books
	rococo an elaborate style of architecture, decoration and furniture-making
431	**credo** a belief or a set of beliefs; from credo (Latin), I believe
433	*coup de grâce* death blow
434	**anathema** an ecclesiastical curse meaning banishment
435	**Christina Rossetti** (1830–94) English poet, sister of Dante Gabriel Rossetti
437	**Chopin** Frederic Chopin (1810–82), Polish composer and pianist
	mazurka a lively Polish dance
	dactyl a word or words comprising three syllables, with the accent on the first

QUESTION

In what ways does the first ending (Chapter 44) compare and contrast with the second ending (Chapter 60)?

CHAPTER 61

 CHECK THE BOOK

Linda Hutcheon argues that hope for a union 'is rendered vain in Arnold's poem by "A God" and in Fowles's novel by three gods – Sarah, the narrating novelist and Fowles – whose various worlds each logically allow only this ending in structural, artistic terms and in thematic, moral ones' ('The "Real World(s)" of Fiction: *The French Lieutenant's Woman*', p. 132).

- The narrator enters the story in a different guise.
- He observes the house and puts back his watch fifteen minutes.
- The action reverts to the point where Charles talks of the dagger in his breast.
- Now Charles sees Sarah as a deceiver, refuses to be detained and leaves the house.
- His final thoughts suggest that he has found some faith to sustain him in an uncertain future.

The narrator observes the house where Sarah is lodging. He now has the appearance of 'the successful impresario'. He takes out his watch and adjusts the time back by fifteen minutes. He then leaves in his landau.

The action reverts to the point where Charles accuses Sarah of planting 'the dagger in my breast' (p. 433). As before, Charles turns to leave. He accuses Sarah of cruelty. Again she refuses to listen to him, but her smile and her eyes seem to suggest a solution. Charles realises that Sarah cannot sacrifice her spirit. He realises that he has been manipulated. As he finally leaves, he sees the girl with the small child in her arms, but he refuses to be detained.

In the deserted street he notices a landau turning the corner. He realises that he must begin life anew, possibly returning to America. He sees a movement of the curtains in the house, but this is only an effect of the wind. Sarah looks down from the studio window at the young woman and the child in the garden. It remains uncertain who exactly the child is and quite what Sarah feels.

Charles is left to consider his future without Sarah, but with some 'atom of faith in himself' in a hostile world.

COMMENTARY

The first phase of the final chapter is the reappearance of the narrator, now no longer the Victorian novelist but a much-changed figure. There is a distinction in the pronouns used, indicating two different personalities at work here: 'I did not want to introduce him'. Moreover, the 'he' seems to have asserted his will, nevertheless, in that he 'has got himself in' – into the novel and this time into Cheyne Walk (pp. 440–1). Fowles's **ludic subversion** continues in the qualities he ascribes to this figure. Before we get to the rather absurd details of the 'impressario', we have the self-mockery of this narrator, 'the sort of man who cannot bear to be left out of the limelight'. Insistence (italicised for emphasis) that this is '*as he really is*' suggests that this modern narrator figure is a true picture. The beard is now foppish and Frenchified (an amused hint of Alain Robbe-Grillet rather than Thackeray). The distinction between physical appearances may also be a distinction in literary styles, the one seen as 'preaching', the other as 'grand opera'. The didacticism and God-like omniscience of the Victorian is replaced by a different, somewhat casual manipulator, who 'cannot contain his amusement' and regards what he sees as material for use 'as if some new theatre he has just bought'. The God-like figure, however, remains, as he has a 'proprietary air' and 'evidently regards the world as his to possess and use as he likes'.

The suggestion that more important business awaits him, coupled with his jaunty disappearance in the landau, leans towards the idea that this may be Fowles himself, the novelist, setting out on a new writing project, as this one is ready to be left to complete itself.

The turning back of the watch is his last action before departing. Immediately, we have a cinematic 'cut', a rewind of the camera, and the scene replays from the same moment ('No it is as I say ...', pp. 433 and 442). The nature of the conversation is now much altered, and the scene plays to a very different conclusion, with Charles and Sarah the ones determining the outcome, independent of the disappearing impresario. Sarah's enigmatic smile suggests a meaning elusively just out of reach, just beyond Charles's immediate perception. However, Charles's refusal to accept Sarah's

CHECK THE BOOK

Dwight Eddins suggests that Charles's 'final plunge into the city's "iron heart" is the reader-persona's plunge from the comfort of an ordered Victorian metaphor, into the unadorned chaos of reality' ('John Fowles: Existence as Authorship' in Pifer, ed., *Critical Essays on John Fowles*, p. 52).

CHECK THE BOOK

The final paragraph of *The French Lieutenant's Woman* has been compared to the endings of earlier modern novels and a Victorian novel. Read the final paragraphs of each of the following novels: *A Portrait of the Artist as A Young Man* (1913) by James Joyce; *Sons and Lovers* (1913) by D. H. Lawrence; and *Moby Dick* (1851) by Herman Melville.

'In the last ending, past and future merge into the present moment. Charles walks out of the residence of Dante Gabriel Rossetti with no preconceived ideas about his future, knowing that every step he will take from now on will be the result of a personal, though difficult, choice' (Onega, *Form and Meaning in the Novels of John Fowles*, p. 91).

offer of a Platonic relationship on her terms is an indication of his growth towards self-understanding, self-sufficiency in spite of loss – in short, selfhood, something that perhaps Sarah has understood.

The image of 'a black avalanche' (p. 444) suggests a kind of suffocating death, rather different from the landslide that 'engulfed' him in the second meeting with Sarah in the shifting rock strata of the Undercliff (p. 140). Charles's future lies elsewhere. The narrator, like Sarah possibly at the window, 'too far away for me to tell', cannot comment. Charles has left behind him Sarah and the Victorian ideologies of duty, the gentleman's honour and traditional values, but has gained 'an atom of faith in himself'. The reader is invited to contemplate Charles's possible 'foolishness' and Sarah's 'battle for territory', which result in their separation and isolation. However, the invitation that 'you may think' is stopped short by the imperative: 'But what you must not think is that this is a less plausible ending to their story' (p. 445).

The return, in the penultimate paragraph, to the epigraphs to Chapter 61 draws attention to two vital considerations. The first epigraph, which suggests that God is the interaction between chance and nature, supports Fowles's belief in the lack of 'an intervening god' beyond 'chance'. However, Fowles does offer something more than a bleakly tragic view of Fate, Hardy's distant President of the Immortals or the Immanent Will. The existential 'atom of faith' alludes to the 'nucleic acid helix' in the epigraph and suggests that there is a way to exist in a bleak, lonely universe. John Donne's poem is reversed in the assertion that we are all 'enisl'd', and this bleakness is captured in the adverbs and adjectives in the image of the final sentence. Life is not to be abandoned, 'but is to be, however inadequately, emptily, hopelessly into the city's iron heart, endured. And out again, upon the unplumb'd, salt, estranging sea.' In the midst of the bleakness, two glimmers of hope are present: first in the verb 'endured', and second, in the determination of 'out again'; the first in the here and now, the second in the future and elsewhere. Arnold's short poem (quoted on p. 408) is another of the echoes in the ending, reaffirming both Charles's isolation and his freedom.

GLOSSARY

440	**chloral** a colourless, oily liquid, used as a sedative and fatal if taken in excess
441	**panatella** a long, thin cigar
	malachite a green mineral
	flânerie idling, time-wasting
441	**Breguet** Abraham-Louis Breguet (1743–1823), Swiss manufacturer of clocks and watches
	landau a horse-drawn carriage with a folding top
443	**Platonic** affectionate, but not involving sexual relations
	soupirant a suitor (French)

 QUESTION

The final question is concerned with the involvement of the reader as an active participant in the narrative. What were your thoughts as you read the two final endings and in particular the last paragraph of *The French Lieutenant's Woman*?

EXTENDED COMMENTARIES

TEXT 1 – CHAPTER 10, PP. 73–5

From 'Charles stood in the sunlight ...' to end of chapter.

This meeting with Sarah in the Undercliff is the first time that Charles has come across her alone since he first saw her on the Cobb in Chapter 1. His first reaction, an echo of sensationalist Victorian fiction, is that he has come across a corpse. The image of the corpse or the fear that Charles will find a dead woman is repeated several times in the **narrative**, for example in Carslake's Barn as Charles anticipates some 'atrocious mutilation, a corpse' beyond the partition.

This particular situation is important in a number of ways. From a narrative point of view, we have already seen the effect of shock that the name Ware Commons has on Mrs Poulteney at the end of the previous chapter. The link with Charles's geological expedition is made as we have just been told that the Undercliff is a part of Ware Commons, though we have yet to connect the reputation of the place with Charles's being there and now stumbling across Sarah.

The position occupied by the sleeping woman is literally dangerous, but it is in the extended metaphorical sense that the word 'fall' is

CHECK THE NET

For examples of the Pre-Raphaelite use of natural background, visit **www. excelsiordirect. com/pre-raph.htm**. Here you will find paintings that provide a rich example of iconography in the Pre-Raphaelite style.

developed throughout the book. The **iconography** of the images – 'the sunlight', the flowers, 'the vivid green clumps of marjoram' ready to 'bloom'– that lie behind him in the 'tiny alpine meadow' is reminiscent of Pre-Raphaelite and Renaissance art forms. Before him is the woman and the 'sheer drop of some thirty or forty feet into an ugly tangle of brambles', and then 'the real cliff plunged down to the beach'. The image of Sarah asleep on the ledge, 'a scattered handful of anemones around her', produces another striking visual image. Both are reminiscent of the paintings of the Pre-Raphaelites, perhaps a foreshadowing of later events in the story, when Sarah's future life is wound up with the artists of this group in London. There is also a suggestion of Milton's Eve awakening in the Garden of Eden. The biblical allusion will be followed by a significant fall.

Charles's feelings, at first sexual, are replaced by nobler 'fraternal, perhaps paternal feelings' in considering Sarah's apparent innocence, her 'being unfairly outcast' and her 'appalling loneliness'. This will not be the first time that Charles displays ambivalent feelings towards Sarah, revealing an inner conflict of emotions or understandings that are a part of his incompleteness in the Jungian sense.

It is at this point, as Charles is looking closely at her, that she wakens. Again, the actual communication is limited to a few moments, this time to Charles's brief, embarrassed apology. As he makes his way up the path, there is a sense of a not quite fulfilled epiphany for Charles in the specificity of the moment – 'above the waiting sea, in that luminous evening silence broken only by the waves' quiet wash, the whole Victorian age was lost'. The narrator significantly places the incident into a broader perspective with the final emphatic comment, 'And I do not mean that he had taken the wrong path.'

The motif of paths and the metaphorical suggestion of choice permeate the **narrative**, not only in the choice of path that Charles makes literally in the Undercliff, but further in the choices he makes in life, still further in the decisions in the context of the Victorian age, and further still in the choices faced by the narrator and ultimately by the novelist. Several brief encounters in the novel, like this one here, are moments in time in which destinies are altered.

TEXT 2 – CHAPTER 39, PP. 296–8

From 'In the street …' to end of chapter.

This incident follows immediately from Charles's leaving the Terpsichore club, where he has witnessed a grotesque sex show and prostitutes at work. His ambivalent feelings include revulsion and a mixture of sexual irritation and excitement. As he blunders out into the street, he hails a cab and calls out the name of a street near to his home – as was the custom of Victorian gentlemen anxious to hide their involvement with the seedier aspects of the city.

In one sense Charles shows the gentleman's acceptance of heavy drinking, prostitution and the exploitation of women, yet he is not typical. He questions himself ('Where now was the travelled man of the world?'). He feels unnatural, comparing himself to his father who 'had lived a life in which such evenings were a commonplace'. The word 'intolerable', used directly twice on page 297, runs through this sequence, expanded by a cluster of words that start with 'He did not feel nobly decent'. This feeling is extended in the gentlemanly terms of 'swallowed an insult' and 'funked a duel'. It is a more personal dilemma in the recurrent motifs of entrapment and emergent existentialist freedom ('a prisoner', 'a dream that he was free' and the 'black reality of his cell'). Even more personal is the wish to punish himself, and the recollection of Sarah and the deliberate drawing of blood from the thorn tree in the Undercliff. A subliminal reference to Sarah lies in the word 'lance', a reminder of that look and all is connotations – reproving, accusatory, assertive, sexual.

The interlude in the street enables the narrator to show the reality of street prostitution in the Victorian era, the world occupied by young women such as the one that Charles eventually picks up. The street being 'crowded with other hansoms and carriages' and the fact that 'under each light, in every doorway stood prostitutes' indicates the extent and acceptance of prostitution in Victorian times. Later in the incident, thoughts of disease, perhaps more likely

CHECK THE BOOK

Thomas C. Foster points out aspects of the language and syntax in the conclusion to the chapter: 'Readers will instantly recognize the rhetoric of sexual seduction in this passage, with its breathless pause, its lapping of waves – long the cinematic cliché for sexual climax – and in the overstatement of an age being lost. Charles has most certainly started down a different kind of wrong path' (*Understanding John Fowles*, p. 75).

from 'a mere Cockney streetwalker', bring a further touch of harsh reality to the problem. The girl's reassurance about 'worries like that', seen as 'an oblique answer to his fears', indicates an awareness about Charles's thoughts of disease that cuts across the pathos. The epigraph to the chapter, a letter of 1854 to *The Times* from an anonymous prostitute, gives voice to the problem and its causes and a different meaning to the concept of 'disease'.

Thoughts of Sarah are again evoked as Charles notices the 'auburn hair', the 'alert dark-shadowed eyes' and the 'vaguely wistful stance' of the girl in the street. The resemblance is an illusion, the hair 'too red to be natural'. However, it is almost as if Charles is searching for something beyond 'just a tinge' of similarity in the tentative 'something in the firm eyebrows, perhaps, or the mouth'. Later in the incident, at the prostitute's rooms, further parallels of coincidence connect Charles and two images of Sarah in his life.

QUESTION

In this incident and the ones immediately surrounding it (the scenes in Ma Terpsichore's and in the prostitute's rooms), what is your opinion of Charles's ambivalent attitudes?

The pathos of the solitary girl is expressed in the fact that 'she seemed forlorn, too inexperienced'. It is emphasised in the 'cheap perfume', and 'the light cloth' of her dress in the 'terrible cold' of the night. Her brief history of two years since she was eighteen is cruelly juxtaposed with the terribly dispassionate 'mathematics' of her possible clients. The 'two years' motif is a coincidental link with the idea of time in the novel – Charles's parents' marriage before the death of mother and stillborn sister, the two years in exile from Sarah, Fowles's two years of 'gestation' of the book. There is pathos, too, in the brief, almost polite exchange between Charles and the girl, even enhanced by the 'tiny hesitation' about the price, which was 'pathetically dishonest', the adverb possibly intended in both senses of the word.

William Palmer suggests that, having portrayed 'one gathering of pornographers' at Ma Terpsichore's , Fowles is able to explore a theme of the book, 'the juxtaposition of pornography to reality'. This theme will develop as the action continues with the scenes in the prostitute's rooms.

TEXT 3 – CHAPTER 55, PP. 388–90

From 'For a while…' to end of chapter.

We have already seen direct comment from the narrator intruding into the story and the shock of direct confession, recognised as playful illusion, about his control of characters and God-like omniscience. Now the appearance of the narrator is made flesh, as it were, as he boldly steps into the story and into the railway carriage. The **ludic subversion** enters a new context.

This appearance is not quite in the manner of Henry Fielding, who climbs into a coach with the reader of *Tom Jones*. In *The French Lieutenant's Woman* the narrator joins one of his characters in a scene reminiscent of Pirandello or even the signature walk-on part of the director Alfred Hitchcock in his own films.

The portrayal of the 'massively bearded' stranger is self-**parody**, extended in the image of the narrator as 'not quite a gentleman … an ambitious butler (but butlers did not travel first class) or a successful lay-preacher'. The suggestion in 'prophet-bearded' is that this man may be able to see into the future, which of course, in the manner of the omniscient narrator, he can. However, he plays the game of a **postmodernist** narrator wondering what to do with the character.

The purpose of the intrusion is to continue to 'dispel his own illusion', as Huffaker puts it in his critique. The narrator abandons the God-like omniscience. However, this in itself is an illusion, for we have the admission that this is pretence ('I have pretended to slip back into 1867') and that any freedom is limited since 'we know what has happened since'. Mocking the 'omnipotent god' with the aside 'if there were such an absurd thing', the narrator also mocks the avant-garde ideas of the *nouveau roman* whose representative in this chapter is portrayed as having a 'mean and dubious … moral quality'.

The tone of the passage is conversational, drawing the reader, the *hypocrite lecteur* of Baudelaire, into a confidence, almost collusion with the author. He addresses the sleeping Charles – 'Now what

CHECK THE FILM

The film of *The French Lieutenant's Woman* replicates the illusory nature of art as well as the role of the impresario, narrator, novelist and film-maker in relation to the characters.

CHECK THE BOOK

Robert Huffaker's comments on the narrator's entrance into the carriage suggest that 'he is incognito as the archetypal Victorian novelist. Like Thackeray, he is "prophet bearded," "the bullying 'tabernacle' preacher" … with the look of an omnipotent god' (*John Fowles*, p. 105).

CHECK THE BOOK

Fowles comments on *keraunos* or pure hazard in life, whose 'results may be hoped for, expected, predicted, dreaded; but they are never certain, *real*, until after they have occurred'. He adds that *keraunos* makes a nonsense of 'that dark iron necessity, the arrow of time' ('The Nature of Nature', in *Wormholes*, p. 347).

CHECK THE BOOK

Katherine Tarbox comments on Fowles's refusal to 'fix the fight' and control his readers: 'He refuses, in effect, to collect his readers. He desires in his fiction to allow the reader the same psychoanalytic, reconstructive experience as the protagonist, with its attendant, sometimes uneasy freedoms' (*The Art of John Fowles*, p. 9).

could I do with you?' – and then, following the more colloquial and revealing 'what the devil am I going to do with you?', shares his problem and possible solution with the reader. The reader watches the narrator/novelist at work on a problem. The use of the present and past tense in 'the conventions of Victorian fiction allow, allowed no place for the open ending' points to the double perspective of time in *The French Lieutenant's Woman*, which now has a twentieth-century narrator in the physical body of a Victorian narrator.

To further play with the reader's expectations and involvement, the narrator will offer two further endings, and hazard will decide which will come first. This, too, is a playful illusion, a **ludic subversion** of the narrative, since only the narrator knows on which side the coin falls. The disclaimer that he will not take part in 'fixing the fight' is disingenuous, though the statement 'so strong is the tyranny of the last chapter, the final, the "real" version' suggests that the second of these will be the narrator's choice.

The moment of choice is deliberate, captured in the repeated 'I' performing with a series of precise verbs the act of tossing the coin: 'I take … I extract … I rest … I flick … and catch'. The reader's hopes, however, are dashed for all we get is 'So be it'. Is this a mocking bow to the omniscient god, for in biblical terms 'so be it' is translated as 'amen'?

There is an amusing piece of self-mockery in the suggestion that the narrator is like 'some invisible speck of dirt (a surrogate for myself)' on the nap of Charles's hat. Charles wakes, unaware that his future, may have been decided while he slept. This is a multi-faceted implicit comment about freedom: the freedom accorded to characters is set alongside determinism; the avant-garde **postmodernist** narrator is set alongside his omniscient Victorian counterpart. Finally, we have the modernist disappearance of the author, who, in a manner that James Joyce would have commended, abruptly leaves Charles. The concrete and final sentence 'The bearded man has disappeared into the throng' is a metaphor for the postmodernist author leaving his story to unfold to its double conclusion without his fixing the fight.

PART THREE

CRITICAL APPROACHES

CHARACTERISATION

Though the central action of the **narrative** is driven by the triangle of relationships between Charles Smithson, Sarah Woodruff and Ernestina Freeman, *The French Lieutenant's Woman* is populated by a number of lesser, but no less interesting characters, who contribute to the evocation of the mid Victorian age in a provincial seaside town. Other 'real' characters also briefly enter the fictional world, notably in the Cheyne Walk sequence when Sarah is found among the Pre-Raphaelites. Finally, there is one other significant character who has featured as a voice throughout the narrative, but who finally steps into his own story and the railway carriage in Chapter 55. This is the narrator of the story. In the final chapter, somewhat changed, he reappears in Cheyne Walk, adjusts his watch and allows Charles and Sarah to work out their own conclusions to their story. With other things on his mind, perhaps another story, he gets into his landau and disappears round the bend along the Embankment of the Thames.

SARAH WOODRUFF

Sarah Woodruff is the prime mover of the action in the narrative, though her character is never fully revealed. Her background and her life up to her appointment as governess to the Talbot household is clear enough, but it is her life after the incident with the French lieutenant that is shrouded in rumour, mystery, speculation, judgemental opinion, partial revelations and even deceit.

In her early life Sarah is in many ways a typical young woman of the nineteenth century. Her situation is not unlike that of Tess Durbeyfield in Thomas Hardy's novel *Tess of the d'Urbervilles*. She is born into a poor family, the daughter of a tenant farmer, who, having been given ideas of noble ancestry, seeks to purchase his own farm and educate his daughter so that she will rise out of her low class. Her father falls into debt and dies, having lost his mind, in the

CHECK THE BOOK

Thomas C. Foster speaks of 'Fowles's postmodern gamesmanship', saying, 'He undertakes it in a spirit of great fun. His comments are arch and knowing, his asides are sly, his allusions are diverting, and he brings himself into the novel in two quite different, but equally amusing, guises' (*Understanding John Fowles*, p. 86).

QUESTION

Susana Onega, in *Form and Meaning in the Novels of John Fowles* (p. 83), sees Sarah as being 'presented in wholly literary terms both as "a figure of myth" and as the stereotyped persecuted maiden of Gothic romance'. What evidence can you find for these ideas in the portrayal of Sarah?

CHECK THE BOOK

'Sarah Woodruff remains always out of reach, distant, unknowable, the least fully realized character in the novel, metaphorically out on the quay with her back turned, a reproach to male novelists, perhaps, as well as to her age' (Foster, *Understanding John Fowles*, p. 69).

Dorchester Asylum, leaving Sarah apparently alone in the world. Educated beyond her position in her own society, she becomes a governess, often the only option open to young women such as her. She is thus placed into a higher class, but is unable to participate in it fully.

Sarah's looks conform neither to the Victorian ideal nor to the fashion. She is said to be not beautiful, not even pretty, with 'a strong nose, heavy eyebrows' (p. 74). However, there is something attractive, in both senses of the word, in her face. She has auburn hair, a dark complexion and strong features, but it is the 'fine eyes, dark eyes' that are compelling (p. 75). She seems to be able to see through the guises that other people wear and has a self-composure that hides her own mysteries. Her dress, however, does conform to the Victorian fashion for young women in her position: she wears dark colours, black and indigo, and her hair is tightly tied back. The struggle against conformity is expressed in the 'suppressed intensity of her eyes' and repeated in the 'suppressed intensity of her mouth' (p. 119).

It is Sarah who gives the novel its title, though she insists to Charles on the cruder appellation 'whore' (p. 171). She assumes this self-imposed mantle, apparently deliberately remaining in Lyme and often seen at the end of the Cobb gazing out to sea, a public image of the fallen woman. This image, so dramatically conceived in the book and in the opening sequence of the film, in fact lies at the germination of the novel in Fowles's imagination.

The second part of Sarah's story also bears similarities with the plot of many nineteenth-century novels: a tale of seduction and betrayal. The apparent details of her involvement with the French lieutenant, Varguennes, suggest that he seduces her during his convalescence from injuries sustained in a shipwreck off the coast of Lyme. She follows him to Weymouth, where it is assumed by all and confirmed to Charles by her that the seduction was complete before he deserted her (Chapter 20). Sarah's subsequent dismissal from the Talbot household leaves her virtually destitute and facing a bleak future. However, she is placed, with the support of the vicar of Lyme, in the household of Mrs Poulteney, a mean-spirited and hypocritical widow, whose motives for sheltering Sarah lie in her own desire to be seen as charitable in the eyes of the god she worships and the social circles in which she moves. Sarah's influence at Mrs Poulteney's is positive, bringing a touch of humane understanding to a bleak household (pp. 59–63).

Sarah's involvement with Charles may seem to develop from an interest on his part in her enigmatic qualities, though we are gradually shown that Sarah may have deliberately set up the meetings in order to draw Charles into her world. The eventual climax of the relationship reveals the truth of her affair with Varguennes, most significantly that she remained a virgin (p. 341).

Sarah seeks her own freedom and claims that she is offering Charles a chance to free himself from the constraints of his life and achieve wholeness of being. Her refusal either to lay any guilt against Charles or to allow him to marry her are integral parts of this concern. Her deliberate disappearance seems to have ended any hope for Charles in continuing the relationship.

Her eventual discovery in London two years later living in the household of a member of the Pre-Raphaelite Brotherhood explains how she sees herself in society. Her appearance now is reminiscent of the Pre-Rahaelite image of beauty and her clothing is said to be 'the full uniform of the New Woman' (p. 423). The child that she permits Charles to see may or may not be hers, presenting another, final enigma. Indeed, from the beginning Sarah retains the mysteries of her inner being: hers is the only mind that is not revealed by the narrator.

The two endings offered by the narrator make the reader see Sarah facing a choice. In the first of these (Chapter 60) she can choose reconciliation, probable marriage and a possible compromise of her independence. The second resolution (Chapter 61) offers a sort of independence without marriage, and happiness in a Platonic relationship. She is content to be a secretarial help in the artist's household, seeks no further advancement, seems to have found her niche in a modern society and, in what should be seen as the 'correct' ending (p. 430), again refuses Charles, asserting her own independence and leaving him to face his future without her.

 CHECK THE BOOK
The image of Sarah on the Cobb has similarities with that of Rosanna, another 'fallen woman', who looks out to sea from Cobb's Hole in Wilkie Collins's *The Moonstone* (1868), 'First Period', Chapter 4.

 CHECK THE BOOK
Robert Huffaker sees Sarah as 'the novel's one thoroughly modern character', and says that 'in the Darwinian sense, she is the cultural "missing link" between the centuries – more modern than Victorian' (*John Fowles*, p. 105).

CHARLES SMITHSON

Charles Smithson is seen at the start of the novel as a typical, aristocratic gentleman, of independent means and with ample leisure time in which to pursue his interest in the natural sciences, particularly palaeontology. He has inherited money on the death of his father and fully expects to inherit a further considerable amount and the family title from his uncle, who has remained single all his life. Charles's studies at Oxford were not completed and, though he did play with the idea of joining the Church, his dilettante scientific studies, his life of travel and occasional liaisons with prostitutes abroad seem to have satisfied him. 'Laziness', it is said, was 'Charles's distinguishing trait' (p. 21). His ambivalence towards Victorian values and morality are perhaps symptomatic of the age. He is thirty-two years old and happy not to have been emotionally entangled with women. He has 'outwardly a certain cynicism', which is judged, possibly by Victorian values, to indicate 'inherent moral decay' and his success at charming young ladies is irreverently compared to that of 'a polecat' (p. 22). However, he has been drawn into an engagement with Ernestina Freeman, the daughter of a rich merchant from the rising middle class. The ease with which Ernestina, who sees Charles as a fine match in terms of finance and class, lures Charles into the engagement may also explain his apparent naivety ('too innocent a face, when it was stripped of its formal outdoor mask', p. 46) when faced with Sarah's scheming. Confronted with a drastic change in fortunes on the marriage of his uncle to a younger widow, Charles is in crisis. The offer of a position in Mr Freeman's business is repugnant to the values he has inherited from his privileged position in society, though his motives are more than 'mere snobbism' and range from elements of the 'lazy', the 'cowardly' and the 'frightened' to 'nausea' (p. 284).

Charles has a comfortably superior attitude in his false perception of his evolutionary role in 'the survival of the fittest' (p. 54) and 'the naturally selected' (p. 159). His Darwinism provides him with the vocabulary but not the full understanding of what the terms of the doctrine will mean in the evolution of a social order that is not, as he seems to think, permanent. With his servant Sam, Charles enjoys a relationship based on a kind of schoolboy humour, though there is

CHECK THE BOOK

At the start of the narrative 'Charles Smithson, another lonely Fowlesian orphan, is the conventional hero, a somewhat passive leisured gentleman, an amateur of science in general and fossils in particular, intellectually mildly speculative, living with no larger ambition than that of inheriting a baronetcy from his uncle and marrying the daughter of a very rich draper' (Conradi, *John Fowles*, p. 63).

no doubt about who is in charge (pp. 110–11). There is a pleasant side to Charles in his generosity of spirit, but it is in many ways superficial and dependent on his privileged position. Possibly the best of Charles's kind nature is seen in the incident with the young prostitute and her child, when he displays genuine sympathy and understanding, albeit only for the moment (pp. 308–9).

Charles's attraction to Sarah and increasing involvement with her are cloaked in terms of gallantry to a woman who is both in need and of scientific interest as a puzzling case of female melancholia. This interest is shared with Dr Grogan. There is a conflict in Charles's desire to help Sarah and his awareness of her as an attractive woman. He is drawn deeper into a relationship that is at first innocent, but gradually increases in emotional intensity. He is eventually led into deception, unwilling or unable to reveal to others the details of this improper relationship (p. 144).

The climax of the relationship forces Charles to choose between Sarah and Ernestina. From the first meeting with Sarah in the Undercliff, he has been aware of the social and sexual dangers he is facing, but he is gradually able to overcome his inhibitions and 'engage in the forbidden' (p. 144). Almost as soon as he has committed himself to love of Sarah and abandonment of Ernestina, he discovers that Sarah has deceived him. However, he believes that he and his love can win her. His breaking of the engagement with Ernestina is a drastic step, since it exposes him to loss of reputation, almost certain damaging court action and a future that will be fraught with difficulties (pp. 364–6). His treatment of Ernestina may be seen as callous, but it is clear that she is not the woman to provide him with a life of genuine satisfaction. The values and sense of duty of the stereotypical Victorian gentleman are put aside in his search for emotional fulfilment.

Charles's anguish is encapsulated in the scene in the Exeter church, as he seeks for forgiveness and a meaning to his life (Chapter 48). Of the endings to the story, the only one that suggests a possible completion to his unfinished journey is the last one in Chapter 61. He comes to realise that his future lies in his own development towards full understanding of his own incomplete nature. This

 **CHECK THE BOOK**
David H. Walker says of Charles, 'He finds himself enmeshed in a web of falsehood that increasingly threatens to place him outside the bounds of propriety; not consciously perceiving this danger, he is only too relieved at finding means of avoiding confrontation with Ernestina' ('Remorse, Responsibility, and Moral Dilemmas in Fowles's Fiction', in Pifer, ed., *Critical Essays on John Fowles*, p. 64).

existentialist potential towards wholeness of being that Sarah has awakened takes Charles forward to endure a future without her.

ERNESTINA FREEMAN

At first sight Ernestina is a typically Victorian young lady from a rich, middle-class background. She is pretty in that 'she had the right face for her age'. Its features, 'small-chinned, oval, delicate as a violet', suggest attractiveness (p. 31). However, she can be shallow, spoiled and lacking in taste, which is particularly seen in her plans to transform Winsyatt. Her prime concern has been to attract a suitable husband and she thinks that, in Charles, she has captured the best on offer. Prospects of his inherited wealth and title fulfil her three concerns – marriage, money and social status.

Her refusal to be totally subject to gentlemen and her scheming nature, suggested in the repetition of the 'tilt' at the corners of her eyebrows and her mouth (p. 31), are seen in the way that she ensnares Charles into his proposal. At other times, too, she seems a little false, notably in her reactions to the breaking of the engagement.

Ernestina is seen at her worst in the issue regarding Charles's inheritance. Her plans for aiming to get Winsyatt, her premature ideas for a tasteless renovation and her angry reaction to Charles's loss of the inheritance reveal a mercenary, ambitious vulgarity. She is resentful of Charles's attention to any other woman, even his slight flirtatious, amused attention to Mary, which prophetically touches 'one of her deepest fears about him' (p. 77). The reader's view of her jealousy of Mary is only slightly softened by her gift to Mary of the green dress, which may have had more to do with pleasing Charles after their disagreement over Sam and Mary's courtship than anything else. In this matter of Sam and Mary she is placed in agreement with Mrs Poulteney's condemnation of their behaviour, while, significantly, Charles and Mrs Tranter support the servants (pp. 102–7).

There is some sympathy for Ernestina in the way she is treated by Charles over the broken engagement, especially if this is seen in a Victorian perspective. Her real affection for Charles is apparent, and her intercession with her father not to destroy Charles in the courts

CHECK THE BOOK

Barry N. Olshen views Ernestina as 'amiable, but tedious, intelligent, though only conventionally so, sentimental as opposed to passionate. Her real attraction for Charles, we learn later, was "the ageless attraction of shallow-minded women: that one may make of them what one wants"' (*John Fowles*, p. 73).

CHECK THE BOOK

Marriage in the Victorian era was a vital step for women. Failure to marry would be seen as failure to fulfil one's destiny, and result in a lifetime of dependency. See for example these novels: Anthony Trollope, *He Knew He Was Right* (1869); Amy Levy, *Reuben Sachs* (1888); and Samuel Butler, *The Way of All Flesh* (1903).

shows sympathy and a kind of forgiveness. Ernestina, named after Ernest, her determined father, may have a strength for survival that belies our first impressions of her. Her death on 1 September 1939 (p. 33) indicates a lifetime that has spanned two half-centuries of radical change.

MRS TRANTER

Mrs Tranter, Ernestina's aunt, is one of the most thoughtful and charitable characters in the novel. She is often overlooked in commentaries, but her role in the **narrative** is important as a touchstone for goodness. She is an immediate contrast to the repugnant Mrs Poulteney, a reminder perhaps that not all Victorian mistresses of a household treated their servants as lesser individuals. Her kindness to Mary, akin almost to companionship, her support of Sam and Mary's relationship, her worries about Sarah's disappearance and her concern for Ernestina are unaffected and quietly dignified. Her sense of outrage against Charles's treatment of Ernestina is perfectly understandable in the Victorian, and perhaps even in the modern, context.

DR GROGAN

Dr Grogan is a pleasant, though slightly ambivalent, character. He has many likeable features. Charles is attracted to him in the intellectual and scientific discussions the two are able to engage in. Certainly a pleasant host, he enjoys Charles's male company over drinks and cigars (pp. 158–9). The portrayal of the 'eunuchistic Hibernian' may suggest an Irish bachelor, at ease in the company of women, but not interested in pursuing sexual relationships. He offers Charles well-meaning advice concerning Sarah's behaviour based on his readings of medical cases far beyond the usual interests of a country practitioner in a small town. However, he is rooted in traditional Victorian attitudes, as is seen in his reaction to Charles's breaking of his engagement to Ernestina and his proposal for assigning Sarah to an asylum. The telescope in his study overlooking the bay and his lecherous looks may suggest a slightly voyeuristic aspect to his character (p. 148). In the final analysis, his judgemental view of Charles's actions is softened by his humanity (p. 380) and his recollection of his own past transgressions (p. 379).

 CHECK THE BOOK
Mrs Tranter's attitude towards Mary seems atypical of the Victorian treatment of servants. For some insights into real and literary households, search the index in Judith Flanders's *The Victorian House* (2003), with its many documentary and literary references.

MRS POULTENEY

Mrs Poulteney is a wonderfully unpleasant character of Dickensian grotesqueness, 'like some plump vulture' (p. 25). She is disgracefully superior and cruel, 'like some pagan god' (p. 95), in her attitude to anyone who comes under her influence or her 'eagle eye'. In the name of charity that is totally lacking in her character, she feigns Christian kindness in the hope of impressing a god that she believes will allow her to continue her privileged existence in the hereafter. Her other equally pressing concern is the reputation she has in the eyes of the parochial society in which she operates. Her two obsessions, 'Dirt' and 'Immorality' (p. 25), both appropriately capitalised, and her vivid imaginings of the debaucheries on Ware Commons (p. 94), suggest a disorder in her psychological make-up. The extensive number of servants who have been dismissed by this tyrannical ogress bears witness to her insufferable judgemental hypocrisy. The 'epitome of all the most crassly arrogant traits of the ascendant British Empire', Mrs Poulteney, it is suggested by the twentieth-century **narrative** perspective, would have been worthy of 'a place in the Gestapo' (p. 26). Her virtual defeat by Sarah in the dismissal scene is only matched by her demise in the afterlife, a magnificent piece of Dickensian poetic justice as she falls 'like a shot crow' down to her appropriate, but unanticipated, eternal punishment (p. 326).

MRS FAIRLEY

An appropriate servant to the vile Mrs Poulteney, 'as both women were incipient sadists' (p. 25), Mrs Fairley delights in her attempts to destroy Sarah's life. She is jealous of Sarah's position and the pleasantness she brings into the lives of the servants. Mrs Fairley's willingness to act as a spy for her mean-spirited mistress makes her an ideally unpleasant housekeeper with nothing for us to admire in her warped view of human nature.

SAM FARROW

Sam is the emergent modern man, out for his own interests: apparently honest but in reality self-seeking, sharp, ready to betray (p. 359), even to blackmail. He is prepared to open Charles's mail, steal from him, and spy on him in a possible blackmail plot (p. 330).

He is manipulative, taking advantage of Mrs Tranter's support of Mary, if not of him. However, he is not such a simple stereotype. He has a charm that wins Mary, and their developing romance does have a simplicity and honesty that is lacking elsewhere in the relationships in the novel. His success in the Freeman enterprise (p. 404) is due to a natural flair for the main chance. His ambitions should be seen in the historical perspective of a restrictive age that allows Charles to maintain the status quo and a changing world that allows the entrepreneur to flourish.

Sam does have a conscience, though it must be admitted that he waits for some time before he acts on it and reveals Sarah's whereabouts (p. 405). The question really is about how we judge Sam – in Victorian terms, or those of the twentieth century. Sam Farrow is certainly not the Sam Weller of Charles Dickens's *The Pickwick Papers*, but we should not expect him to be so.

MARY

In many ways Mary is the most attractive of the young women in the novel, a possibility that the narrator asks the reader to consider early on. She represents the simple sexual attraction of womankind with 'an exquisitely pure, if pink complexion, corn-coloured hair and delectably wide blue-grey eyes' (p. 77). While this description may show more than a hint of chauvinistic attitudes, there is no doubt that Mary's 'delighted, self-surprised face' (p. 110) does offer a marked contrast to the 'narcissistic self-contemplation' and repressed sexuality of Ernestina (pp. 34–5), and the darker attractions of Sarah. Healthy and cheerful, Mary's 'mobile, flirtatious surface' is underpinned by 'a gentle affectionateness' and 'warmth' (p. 78).

MR FREEMAN

Ernestina's father is the representative of the increasingly influential middle classes in mid Victorian society. His role in the novel is appropriately conveyed in the reactions of others towards him.

His name is **ironic**, especially when one considers the existential freedom that lies at the heart of the **narrative**. In fact, many of the things connected to Mr Freeman are ironic. Sam works for him largely because he has provided Mr Freeman with valuable

 QUESTION

'Fowles's Sam is, after all, the precursor of the twentieth-century advertising man' (Palmer, *The Fiction of John Fowles*, p. 24). Do you agree with this view of Sam?

 CHECK THE BOOK

Kevin Padian says that 'the aptly named Ernest Freeman is Charles's polar opposite. He has worked, sweated, saved, and conformed in order to build a mercantile empire and gain entrance into an exclusive society. He represents a product of natural selection, adapting successfully to changing environmental conditions over time' ('Deep Time, Evolutionary Legacy, and Darwinian Landscape' in Aubrey, ed., *John Fowles and Nature*, p. 158).

information about Charles. When Sam presents his display of collars with the slogan 'Freeman's for Choice', he seems unaware of the fact that as an employee he himself has little choice but is wholly caught up in a commercial system. Charles senses that he will lose his own sense of freedom if he accepts Mr Freeman's offer of partnership. His rejection of the offer is not simply his desire to remain aloof from the middle classes, but is more to avoid being drawn into the mercenary *nouveau riche* mentality.

Sam's acceptance and Charles's rejection of what Mr Freeman offers is seen largely in **Marxist** terms – 'the actions of men in pursuit of their ends' (p. 445). Mr Freeman is a paradox, though not to himself. In Marxist terms, he contributes 'handsomely to the Society for the Propagation of Christian Knowledge', yet his employees are exploited; in capitalist terms, he has a happy labour force (at least in terms of the mid Victorian age) and yet still has sizeable profits for his heirs (p. 272).

His concern for his daughter seems to be more a matter of pampering her to keep her happy than any genuine care. He does allow her to intercede on Charles's behalf, though this may still be seen in terms of pampering rather than any genuine concern for her or charity towards Charles on his part.

> **CONTEXT**
>
> The rise of the middle classes in the Victorian age did not entirely destroy or undermine landed privilege. Many, like Ernest Freeman, bought into the aristocracy with country houses and estates, thereby consolidating the system and acting as a counter-effect to social revolution.

THEMES

FREEDOM AND CONSTRAINT

The novel presents a number of situations in which constraint affects almost all the characters. The constraint brought about by Victorian law, duty, conventions and ideologies is of several kinds: social, class, religious, moral, sexual, gender and psychological.

Sarah Woodruff is constrained by her upbringing, which has lifted her to a higher level of society that she cannot share in fully. Her post as governess is limiting (pp. 165–6), but her situation in life once she has left that post offers her little other opportunity. Society's conventions and prejudices leave her few choices, but the one choice she can make – to assert her rejection of the values that ostracise her – isolates her. Her claim to have achieved a freedom beyond the pale of Victorian narrowness suggests that she may have defeated the prejudices of the likes of Mrs Poulteney, and the other pillars of Lyme society (p. 171). Her situation at the end of the **narrative** may be seen both as liberation and as another form of limitation of her potential, as she is merely the amanuensis to the artist.

The constraints that work upon Charles take a different form. His privileged position as an English gentleman allows him a freedom to pursue a life of leisured scientific interest and travel, but the loss of wealth and, worse still, transgressions of the socially accepted values of society place him in danger. Involvement with Sarah exposes him to the same disapprobation that she has suffered. The risks he takes in continuing the liaison threaten his fragile engagement to Ernestina, his relationship with her father and his position as a gentleman. Charles is trapped in a dialogue between science and religion, in which his own temporal existence and his scientific training is shown to be inadequate when set against the mysteries of creation, as exemplified in the image of the tiny wren (pp. 233–4). His other dilemma is the choice between 'his last freedom' and his absorption into the Freeman world of commerce. Charles's gradual move towards Jungian individuation, a freedom of wholeness of being beyond the 'iron laws' of Victorian society, is a major aspect of the theme of freedom.

Ernestina is caught in a different social and sexual snare: the Victorian expectations and conventions for young women with regard to marriage and sex. There are glimpses of a certain strength of character beneath the impositions of Victorian demands upon her gender. However, the scene in which she considers her own sexuality expands the Victorian diktat 'I must not', via the Tennyson epigraph and explanatory footnote, to include the whole Victorian dilemma of bodily functions and spiritual concerns. Furthermore, the narrator extends the image of the 'wet blanket' of duty to our own age (pp. 34–5).

Sam and Mary face a different kind of constraint and they desire to escape. The social situation of the underclass of servants was about

CHECK THE BOOK

'In each phase of his self-discovery, Charles surprises. He is both a wealthy Victorian gentleman, aware of social privilege, and an existential hero-in-the-making, sloughing his privileges in order to overcome and create himself anew' (Peter Wolfe, *John Fowles, Magus and Moralist*, 1979, p. 137).

QUESTION

'In one sense *The French Lieutenant's Woman* is a book obsessed with duty,' says Simon Loveday in *The Romances of John Fowles* (p. 63). In what ways does duty affect Charles and Ernestina, and even Sarah in her manipulation of Charles?

CHECK THE BOOK

In the debate between Charles and Dr Grogan, Neil McEwan suggests: 'We see Grogan and Charles as Victorians here, but we are conscious also of their human situation, trapped by history and helpless in time. We sympathise with them as men of their age, and simply as men' (*The Survival of the Novel: British Fiction in the Late Twentieth Century*, 1985, p. 36).

CHECK THE BOOK

'Sarah Woodruff has attained self-hood before the novel even begins. She knows who she is and in her own freedom she knows how to encourage the grasping of freedom by others' (Palmer, *The Fiction of John Fowles*, p. 75).

to change as the nature of Victorian stratified society was challenged by economic, industrial and commercial factors epitomised in the doubly **ironically** named Mr Ernest Freeman, within whose empire Sam achieves a kind of liberation. However, this emancipation still has its constraints, as is made clear in the portrayal of Sam and his family in Chapter 57.

Dr Grogan, too, can be seen as a man caught in time. Likeable, sociable, an emergent Darwinist, he is nevertheless trapped by Victorian conventionality and morality. This is seen in his denouncement of Charles over the affair with Sarah, in spite of his latent sympathies with Charles's dilemma.

EXISTENTIALISM

In *The Aristos* Fowles states that 'Existentialism is the revolt of the individual against all those systems of thought, theories of psychology and social and political pressures that attempt to rob him of his individuality' (*The Aristos*, p. 122). The theme of freedom is very much connected with existentialism in the novel, and the struggle of Sarah and Charles towards liberation is seen in such terms. Responsibility for our own destinies with no god to help or blame means existence in a changing world of legal, moral and social 'laws'. Choices must be made and the free will to make such choices determines whether we accept the 'iron laws' or create our own reality. This post-Victorian philosophy is explored through the emergent existentialists: Sarah, who is said by some to be an existentialist from the beginning, and Charles, who stumbles towards understanding, led by Sarah, but is ultimately alone in making his own choices. Through the angst of his lonely existential suffering, Charles eventually sees, perhaps, what Sarah has known for some time: that the way to move forward in the existentialist void is through self-awareness. This will lead Charles towards, if not to, individuation or wholeness beyond the parameters of the final ending of the book, as he sets out alone on his uncompleted journey with an existentialist 'atom of faith in himself, a true uniqueness on which to build' (p. 445).

EVOLUTION

The figure of Charles Darwin casts its shadow over the Victorian era, threatening the stability of religion and an ordered society. The issue of Darwinism is encapsulated in conversations, notably between Charles and Mr Freeman, and between Charles and Dr Grogan. The language of Darwinism – evolution, adaptation, cryptic coloration, survival of the fittest – permeates the **narrative** in its application to the human condition in a changing society. That evolution is horizontal and not vertical is an understanding that helps Charles perceive his own situation (p. 200).

Mr Freeman is an example of adaptation and survival, as also is Sam at a lower level of the species. Charles's refusal to join the Freeman enterprise is a failure to adapt that may mean that the 'Gentleman' is 'a dying species' (p. 285).

The theme of evolution applies variously in *The French Lieutenant's Woman* to the individual, to society and class, and ultimately to the novel itself and the narrator/author.

TIME

Darwinian thought introduces the idea of deep time, which was a challenge to the Creationist, religious view of man and nature. Geological understandings that added force to the theory of evolution find expression in many of the images in the **narrative**.

Time and space and their shifting nature are not just an aspect of structure, but also a theme within the narrative. The reader is challenged to look at the Victorian milieu from perspectives that go back, for example, to Sappho and Catullus (p. 282) and forward to Alain Robbe-Grillet and Roland Barthes (p. 97). In the years between the nineteenth-century action of the story and the twentieth-century narrative position, several other historical **allusions**, such as reference to the occupancy of houses and to mundane objects like the Toby jug, become a part of the theme.

A further aspect of time is contingency, which may be defined as the way things work out in the future being dependent on other moments in time. Contingency plays a large part in the novels of

QUESTION

In his critique on John Fowles, what do you think Peter Conradi means by the statement: 'Deserted by evolution, he is rescued by existentialism' (p. 75)?

CONTEXT

Fowles believes that 'it is high time we liberated ourselves from the narrow blinkers imposed on us by the notion, both social and scientific, of time as an inexorable onward machine, a clock-wise face we must constantly watch and obey from the moment we first go to school. Psychological time, as every novelist can vouch, is enormously richer and more complex … and more pleasurable' (Foreword by *John Fowles* in Fawkner's *The Timescapes of John Fowles*, p. 130).

Thomas Hardy, but often hinges on fatal coincidence or chance. John Fowles, on the other hand, allows his narrator to tinker with contingency in order to develop the temporal theme. On page 320 and page 328 Sam's question 'Are we stayin' the night?' produces two separate responses from Charles, and the subsequent action turns on these decisions. In Chapter 55 we have the question 'what the devil am I going to do with you?'. The tossing of a coin determines which of two possible contingencies will be revealed first. Finally, in Chapters 60 and 61 we have the same moment, the 'one last second' between Charles and Sarah, played out on pages 433–4 and page 442, leading to two different contingencies. Here the theme of time includes the whole business of writing and the role of the narrator in different ages.

NATURE

Fowles says that nature is the 'key' to his fiction (John Fowles, *The Tree*, 1979, p. 35). Fowles's interest in nature is well documented in his own writings, in interviews and in a collection of critiques that is referred to several times in these Notes (James Aubrey, ed., *John Fowles and Nature*, 1999). The nature theme in *The French Lieutenant's Woman* devolves primarily from the setting in the Undercliff, where what Aubrey terms 'a morally neutral landscape' is found. The theme is explored through Charles's sensibilities, through the view of Sarah as a mythological figure of nature (Eve in the Garden of Eden), and through the natural images of plants and creatures that have their own natural existence but also a symbolic significance, such as the wren (pp. 233–4), a particularly potent example. The theme operates on three levels, in that nature is seen as a force that brings to the character, the reader and the narrator 'a heightened awareness of his or her freedom' (Aubrey, ed., *John Fowles and Nature*, p. 24).

NARRATIVE TECHNIQUE AND LANGUAGE

It has been suggested by many critics that *The French Lieutenant's Woman*, with its metaphorical pathways, was written at an appropriate forking of paths in the history of the British novel. In terms of **narrative**, it breaks new ground and is acknowledged as

---

CONTEXT

'Nearing the almost sub-tropical Undercliff with its luscious vegetation, Charles finds himself enveloped in a sensuous nonhuman world of beautiful organic life. The atmosphere is mysteriously pantheistic, charged with the green energy of unspoiled life, of nature itself' (Fawkner, *The Timescapes of John Fowles*, p. 75).

one of the forerunners of **postmodernist** fiction. Mahmoud Salami summarises the novel's unique quality as its 'narrativisation of history, its intertextuality and its ideological reconstitution of Victorian society'. He points us to the 'multiplicity of narrative voices', which include the author, the narrator and the characters, as well as a narrator-persona who addresses himself directly to the 'reader's persona who is also inscribed into the text' (Mahmoud Salami, *John Fowles's Fiction and the Poetics of Postmodernism*, 1992, p. 105).

Many of the novel's complexities and contradictions stem from the role of the narrator, who comments on character and plot, overtly stops the narration to analyse the freedom from authorship of the characters (Chapter 13), and finally enters his own narrative twice as a walk-on character (Chapters 55 and 61).

Many artists have looked to the past for inspiration, form or style. In *The French Lieutenant's Woman*, there is mention of the Renaissance, a time of massive artistic change in the mid fourteenth to sixteenth centuries, and the Pre-Raphaelite Brotherhood's challenge, on a smaller scale, to traditional values in the nineteenth century. Even though Jean Rhys's *Wide Sargasso Sea* had appeared in 1966, John Fowles may be said to have been the forerunner of a new form for the novel. In its parodic approach to Victorian social, sexual, political and literary conventions, *The French Lieutenant's Woman* looks back one hundred years from a twentieth-century perspective. This approach has since been followed by many writers and may be termed Victorian postmodernism, neo-Victorian or the term coined by Sally Shuttleworth, the 'retro-Victorian novel' ('Natural History: The Retro-Victorian Novel' in Elinor Shaffer ed., *The Third Culture: Literature and Science*, 1998).

In *Possession* (1990), A. S. Byatt speaks of how she has 'ventriloquised' voices of the past, conscious of 'the past persisting in us'. Over twenty years earlier Fowles attempted a similar narrative ploy. In an interview he said, 'In *The French Lieutenant's Woman* I exaggerated the archaic qualities of the language … But you have to give your readers the illusion that they are back in the past' (Robert Foulke, *A Conversation with John Fowles*, 1985–6, p. 376).

CHECK THE NET

A wide-ranging article by Marie-Luise Kohlke on the neo-Victorian novel can be found by following links on **www.neovictorianstudies.com**

CHECK THE BOOK

In *Wide Sargasso Sea* (1966), Jean Rhys tells the story of the mad first wife of Mr Rochester from Charlotte Brontë's *Jane Eyre* (1847).

Fowles was aware of how difficult it was for a writer to 'get the right "voice" for his or her material' and notes a memorandum he wrote for himself: 'You are not the "I" who breaks into the illusion, but the "I" who is a part of it' ('Notes on an Unfinished Novel', in *Wormholes*, p. 18). Fowles synthesises the reconstructed Victorian voices of his characters and that of his narrator, who possesses a twentieth-century awareness and vocabulary.

CHECK THE BOOK

Mahmoud Salami says that 'through the use of epigraphs of various kinds the narrator is able to reconstruct, represent, and "colonise" the cultural milieu of the Victorian age by the representation of aspects of its literary world through the poetry of Hardy, Arnold, Tennyson, and Clough. Other epigraphs that deal with economics, politics, ideology, and the question of sexuality are all expressed in prose' (*John Fowles's Fiction and the Poetics of Postmodernism*, p. 107).

A feature of the novel is embedded quotation and documentary reference in the fabric of the **narrative**. The use of quotation from Victorian authors serves a double purpose: it strengthens the nostalgic Victorian 'feel' of the narrative, and it also reconstructs Victorian literature, culture and ideas for its own purposes, commenting on the Victorian and the modern context at the same time. Documentary passages in the form of other texts such as the La Roncière case, the account of the eighteenth-century brothel show and lengthy footnotes become amusingly subversive when they stretch across a couple of pages (pp. 259–60), break off and then resume on (p. 262 and again on p. 263), deliberately disrupting the traditional narrative and **parodying** their Victorian antecedents.

The first epigraph, from Hardy's poem 'The Riddle', operates at the traditional level of its Victorian antecedents, as an indication of theme as well as literary ornamentation. Other epigraphs acknowledge the significance of eminent Victorian voices from literature, science, and political and philosophical thought. However, it becomes clear that in the Victorian epigraphs, as well as those from other centuries, Fowles is operating at a different level. **Ironic**, parodic, implicit subversive comment means that the epigraphs are assimilated into the neo-Victorian narrative to comment on the age, the narrative and the whole idea of writing itself.

Three elements of narrative style operate in the book. **Pastiche** is evident in the opening paragraph of the book, which imitates the style of Jane Austen; this is particularly appropriate since incidents in *Persuasion* took place on the Cobb. However, the **anachronisms** from the start (in Chapter 1, Henry Moore juxtaposed with Michelangelo) and the amused comment about the 'daring narrowness – and shortness' of the skirt suggest parody

(p. 10). The ironic differences between present and past, the obvious cross-references in time (knowledge of the life-span of the characters, the history of house ownership and the possession of a Toby jug) point to a deliberate **ludic subversion** of the narrative, which laughs in various places at the Victorian tradition, at avant-garde **postmodernist** theory, and even at the self-mocking portraits of the narrator himself in the final chapters (the bearded figure in the train and then the impresario in Cheyne Walk). These three levels of narrative can be traced throughout the book.

We find the emergence of characters who are simultaneously Victorian and un-Victorian. Because of the double narrative perspective, they can be seen as typically Victorian in outlook and also credited with twentieth-century sensibilities. Examples are Charles's existentialism before the term had been introduced (p. 72), and the narrator's interpretation of Sarah's look 'in the modern phrase: Come clean, Charles, come clean' (p. 143). There are several other weavings of twentieth-century perspectives and sensibilities into portrayal of character: mention of the Gestapo in relation to Mrs Poulteney (p. 26) and of the year of the invasion of Poland as the date of Ernestina's death (p. 33), the comparison of Sarah's inner knowledge to a computer (p. 57), the linking of Sam's affectations of style to the mod culture of the 1960s (pp. 46–7), and so on.

In the central character of the novel, emphasis is place on the outcast in Victorian society. In a superficial way her position reflects that of many other Victorian protagonists. Jane Eyre, Tess, Oliver Twist and others along with Sarah Woodruff offer a means of criticising social attitudes and values.

There is a development from the Victorian novel, however, in the treatment of sex and sexuality. Fowles himself has said that almost all the Victorians with the exception of the later Hardy failed to deal with the actions, the words and the emotions of the most intimate moments of sex. *The French Lieutenant's Woman* can be seen as a comment on the sexual hypocrisy of the Victorian age. Several incidents foreground Victorian attitudes to sexuality: Ernestina's thoughts in her room (pp. 34–5) and, equally importantly, the footnote on page 35 that qualifies the chapter's epigraph from

CHECK THE BOOK

'In reflecting on the literary past, novels are often seen to be reflecting on the three-way relations between novels, other novels, and the history that connects and divides them. In engaging with their literary precedents, such novels engage with the history of beliefs and attitudes to which those originals belonged and which they have helped to shape' (Steven Connor, *The English Novel in History 1950–1999*, 1996, p. 167).

QUESTION

How successfully does Fowles present differing attitudes towards sexuality in *The French Lieutenant's Woman*?

In Memoriam; the ostracism of Sarah and the attitudes of Lyme society; the incident with the young London prostitute (Chapters 39–41), and the consummation of the sexual act between Charles and Sarah (Chapter 46). The inclusion of the eighteenth-century account of the brothel (pp. 293–5) is central to the **parody** of the respectable Victorian novel, since it replaces the omission of such scenes in the 1867 **narrative**. The narrator's explicit comment on the difference between 1749 and 1867 and the auctioning off of the girls in the final tableau completes the intention of the parody.

Because they were frequently published in serial form, many Victorian novels had cliff-hanger endings to each episode, much like present-day soap operas. *The French Lieutenant's Woman* consciously imitates this form, often deliberately moving the action in time and place and keeping the reader waiting for an answer for some time. This **pastiche** of the suspense of the Victorian novel leads into a parodic dimension. We are kept waiting for a full chapter to discover along with Charles, as he 'craned fearfully over the partition' in the barn, what horror lay waiting (Chapters 35–7). The parody is accentuated in the novel's open endings that subvert the tradition of narrative closure. The two (three, if we count the neat Romantic conclusion of Chapter 44) versions of closure refute the Victorian model in which loose ends are neatly tied up. Instead the onus is placed on the reader as participant in the fiction and granted his or her own freedom of choice by a narrator who says, 'If this is a novel, it cannot be a novel in the modern sense of the word' (Chapter 13, p. 97).

In these phases of the novel the Victorian omniscient narrative is juxtaposed with a **postmodernist metafiction** where, in the words of Alain Robbe-Grillet, 'Invention and imagination have finally become the subject of the book' (*'Snapshots' and 'Towards a New Novel'*, trans. Barbara Wright, 1965, pp. 46–7).

The shock of Chapter 13 is the obvious reference it makes in this respect. Here we are told that the narrator cannot control his characters, who have a freedom of their own because of his refusal to be a God-like omniscient narrator. The new God is the existentialist idea of 'freedom that allows other freedoms to exist'

(p. 99). The first section of the chapter is a parody of an analysis of the creative process and a blurring of the distinctions between reality and illusion. The parody, however, extends to the narrator's own analysis, his own creative process, when he abruptly launches into an omniscient, metaphorical account of Sarah's 'long fall'.

This freedom of the narrator introduces the question of deceit in the structure of the narrative, which is, in fact, constructed around one central lie. Sarah has never been the 'woman' of the French lieutenant and has constructed her own fiction within the fiction of the novel. Her deceit in some ways resembles the deceit of the narrator: both are using the necessary means to present their stories and draw attention to their situations.

IMAGERY AND MOTIFS

Some central features of the language of *The French Lieutenant's Woman* are referred to above in relation to the double perspective of a century's difference in time. Other important aspects lie in the rich imagery and recurrent **motifs** of the narrative. The Undercliff presents simultaneously abundant natural images, particularly of birds and plants (Chapter 10 is a good example, and there are several passing references elsewhere), and the thematic idea of the Garden of Eden. Sarah's presentation as what Susan Onega has termed 'the Green Woman', a kind of natural embodiment of Nature, is set against a backdrop of woods and landslips. Natural images of pathways and forks in the path lead to metaphorical suggestions of choice, while the dangers of the paths on the high cliffs link with the idea of falling in all its interpretations (pp. 74–5). The natural imagery of lightning and approaching storm (pp. 198 and 217) is complemented by an existentialist 'flash of black lightning' (p. 200).

Frequent geological and Darwinian references enter into the imagery, notably time, fossils, stratification, adaptation and survival. These **allusions** thus serve a double purpose that is both thematic and linguistic. Charles is frequently seen (or sees himself) as a fossil, trapped in time (pp. 281 and 350). Appropriately, in the location

CHECK THE BOOK
'John Fowles is one of the few writers whom one may call a lover of nature without being trite. His deep love keeps both him and his stories always near green solitudes. He and his wife Elizabeth live an unperturbed country life in Lyme Regis ... The lush garden around their big eighteenth-century rococo house is the sort of private *"domaine"*, *"sacred combe"* or *"bonne vaux"* so prominent in his fiction – and so obviously necessary to his life' (Huffaker, *John Fowles*, p. 15).

CHECK THE BOOK

Speaking of the power of words over the visual imagery of the cinema, Fowles says, 'A sentence or paragraph in a novel will evoke a different image in each reader. This necessary cooperation between writer and reader – the one to suggest, the other to make concrete – is a privilege of verbal form; and the cinema can never usurp it' (*Wormholes*, p. 24).

of the story, the danger he faces is often seen in terms of an abyss (p. 143), a landslide (p. 140) or an avalanche (p. 444).

Mirrors are a recurrent **motif** featured, for example, with Ernestina (p. 34), Charles (pp. 45–6) and Sarah (p. 269). These scenes offer insights into character as well as comparison and contrast between characters and situations. The physical mirror images also point to the many structural reflections and parallels in the novel, notably Sarah on the Cobb in Chapter 1 and Charles on the promontory in Chapter 59 (p. 416). In the 1981 film version, use of mirrors picks up the the idea of self-examination and illusion in the Victorian age, as well as the mirroring of the past century in the present.

The novel begins and ends with images of the sea. Besides the shipwreck that brought the French lieutenant to Sarah, other incidental images of ships on the horizon are part of the scenic, naturalistic world that Fowles creates (pp. 96 and 123). As the story moves to its conclusion, the image of islands and 'the unplumb'd, salt, estranging sea', drawn from Arnold's 'To Marguerite' (quoted on pages 408–9), reinforce the existentialist theme. Charles, in his involvement with Sarah, is portrayed as 'beset by a maze of cross-currents, swept hopelessly away from his safe anchorage' (p. 172) and, in his final rejection, with 'his masts crashing, the cries of the drowning in his ears' (p. 438).

Some of Fowles's linguistic **allusions** are almost subliminal, even throwaway, so that the reader comes across them, if not exactly by chance, then by a retrospective discovery. These intentional images, such as the easily missed 'pet donkey' (p. 443) or the more obvious wren (pp. 223–4), contribute to a dense text, rich in **allusion** and imagery.

PART FOUR

CRITICAL PERSPECTIVES

READING CRITICALLY

This section provides a range of critical viewpoints and perspectives on *The French Lieutenant's Woman* and gives a broad overview of key debates, interpretations and theories proposed since the novel was published. It is important to bear in mind the variety of interpretations and responses this text has produced, many of them shaped by the critics' own backgrounds and historical contexts.

No single view of the text should be seen as dominant – it is important that you arrive at your own judgements by questioning the perspectives described, and by developing your own critical insights. Objective analysis is a skill achieved through coupling close reading with an informed understanding of the key ideas, related texts and background information relevant to the text. These elements are all crucial in enabling you to assess the interpretations of other readers, and even to view works of criticism as texts in themselves. The ability to read critically will serve you well both in your study of *The French Lieutenant's Woman*, and in any critical writing, presentation, or further work you undertake.

CRITICAL RECEPTION

The French Lieutenant's Woman was released in the United Kingdom on 12 June 1969. When Fowles completed the novel and sent it to his editor Tom Maschler, he declared, 'You won't like it.' Maschler's 'magnificent' telegram and the offer of a large advance surprised Fowles, though there was some ambivalence in the author's mind about the financial reward and the recognition of his achievement.

The initial critical reception in the British press of 12 June 1969 was mixed – 'bouquet and reservation', as Fowles termed it. Praise such as 'rewarding' from the novelist William Trevor in *The Guardian*

CHECK THE BOOK

A diary entry for 27 October 1967 about completion of *The French Lieutenant's Woman* reads: 'I finished the first draft, which was begun on 25 January. It is about 140,000 words long, and exactly as I imagined it: perfect, flawless, a lovely novel. But that, alas, is only how I imagine it.'

CONTEXT

Eileen Warburton, quoting Fowles from his diaries, writes, 'When he won the W. H. Smith Prize (1970) and the Silver Pen Award (1969) for *The French Lieutenant's Woman*, he was embarrassed. Returning from his 1969 American tour, Fowles was surprised to discover himself the prizewinner for the "English Circle of International PEN, whatever that is", since he had not known he was short-listed. Disapproving, "on principle", of literary prizes, he wanted to turn it down, but "Tom Maschler has already been to a dinner and accepted it for me"' (*John Fowles*, p. 337).

was qualified by the idea that 'symbols and allegory stain almost every page of this long and puzzling book'. However, *The Observer*'s Stephen Wall felt that the book was 'a remarkable performance as well as an interesting exercise' and the *New Statesman*'s James Price believed that Fowles had produced 'a splendid, lucid, profoundly satisfying work of art'. D. A. N. Jones in the *Times Literary Supplement* said that Fowles had managed 'in this tour de force, to emulate the great Victorians'. In the *Daily Telegraph* Elizabeth Berridge also termed the novel 'a tour de force', though felt that the reader might be 'vastly beguiled and/or irritated' by its complexity.

Advanced reviews of the novel in November 1969 from the United States, however, were more than favourable and the book quickly went into a third American printing. It became a Literary Guild selection that topped and remained in the best-selling lists in *Time* magazine and the *New York Times* for over a year. A partial explanation for the different reaction in the United States is provided in the Warburton biography (p. 317; see pp. 313–15 for Fowles's reactions to the mixed British reviews). The novel was particularly well received on the campuses of American universities, which possibly accounts for the range of critical works that followed in the seventies and eighties. *Time* magazine said it was 'richer and more accomplished than *The Collector* or *The Magus*', while Ian Watt, in the *New York Times* review of 20 November 1969, found it 'immensely interesting, attractive and human' as well as 'both richly English and convincingly existential'.

The dichotomy between the favourable American reviews and the mixed ones in Britain did not prevent the novel from winning awards: the Silver PEN Award in 1969 and the W. H. Smith Prize in 1970. Moreover, the popularity of the film adaptation of *The French Lieutenant's Woman* in 1981 seemed to alter the tenor of British comment, and certainly British sales had exceeded one million by 1984. Nevertheless, it was from American sources that the bulk of critical analysis was to come.

RECENT CRITICISM

In the forty years since *The French Lieutenant's Woman* was published, there has been a wealth of critical writing on John Fowles. Many of the books and essays have been produced in the United States, where his work has always been popular with the general reading public, in colleges and universities, and with academic scholars.

The range of criticism on *The French Lieutenant's Woman* is varied, from the earlier traditional approaches to styles developed in the **postmodernist** period. The attempt to pigeon-hole critical approaches, especially with a multi-layered text such as *The French Lieutenant's Woman*, is unwise, since many critics acknowledge other aspects of critical approach in the main thrust of their enquiry. You should keep this in mind as you examine critical works and formulate your own thoughts on and responses to the novel. Discussion of some of the critical works noted in this section is developed further in **Contemporary approaches** to help form the basis for your critical reading of the novel.

A good starting point for some of the earlier critical approaches is *John Fowles: A Reference Companion* by James R. Aubrey, which deals with several aspects of Fowles's work, including a short account of critical approaches up to 1990. *Critical Essays on John Fowles*, edited by Ellen Pifer, offers a selection of essays on John Fowles, including Linda Hutcheon's 'The "Real World(s)" of Fiction: *The French Lieutenant's Woman*', as well as an index that directs you to relevant references in other essays. James Acheson's *John Fowles* (1998) is a good guide to Fowles's early novels.

One of the first critical works to appear was Elizabeth Rankin's 1973 critique, 'Cryptic Coloration in *The French Lieutenant's Woman*', which sees the novel's essential concern to be with existential freedom, beneath what she terms a 'smokescreen' that presents Fowles's didactic messages in the **narrative**. 'Cryptic coloration' is the Darwinian term for the means of survival of animals by concealment or by blending with their surroundings, but

CONTEXT

John Fowles was struck by the amount of critical attention given to his work. In a BBC *Bookshelf* interview with Frank Delaney, he said, 'The most horrible and shocking thing that's happened to me recently was to receive not a very small book, a book I suppose that must have been half an inch thick, and that is simply a bibliography about my work. And three quarters of which I've never read' (quoted by James R. Aubrey, *John Fowles: A Reference Companion*, 1991, p. 141).

it clearly applies to humans in their evolutionary adaptation and survival.

Peter Wolfe develops the ideas of the existential search for identity in *John Fowles, Magus and Moralist* (1979). The theme of existential freedom is also explored by William J. Palmer in *The Fiction of John Fowles: Tradition, Art and the Loneliness of Selfhood* (1974). Other early books on Fowles include Barry N. Olshen's *John Fowles* (1978), which provides an account of *The French Lieutenant's Woman* primarily from the perspective of the modern historical novel set in the Victorian age. Another book offering a good overview of Fowles's early work and specific analysis on *The French Lieutenant's Woman* is Peter Conradi's *John Fowles* (1982).

Carol M. Barnum's clear account of Jungian archetypes, *The Fiction of John Fowles: A Myth for our Time* (1985), analyses the ideas of myth and the psychology of character in the novels. It is particularly recommended for its Jungian interpretation of *The French Lieutenant's Woman*. Chapter 4 in *John Fowles* (1980) by Robert Huffaker gives a commentary that covers in seven sub-sections essential features of *The French Lieutenant's Woman*. These sections include an extended summary of the plot, Fowles's position as author/narrator/character, the endings, and the theme of evolution. Huffaker goes beyond seeing a fine historical novel and is one of the early critics to point towards a **postmodernist** view of the **narrative**'s re-creation and **pastiche** of its Victorian antecedents. In addition, the Jungian concept of the anima is applied to Sarah, who aids Charles to self-realisation while at the same time weaving 'a web of fate for herself'.

Simon Loveday in *The Romances of John Fowles* (1985) traces the idea of medieval romance and quest in the fiction of John Fowles. His book connects in some ways with the Jungian analysis of Carol M. Barnum, commenting on psychological archetypes and producing valuable insights into the relationship between Charles and Sarah and the idea of the protagonist's quest. He also develops the Freudian psychological interpretation of Gilbert Rose in his article '*The French Lieutenant's Woman*: The Unconscious Significance of a Novel to its Author' (in *American Imago* 29, 1972).

 CHECK THE BOOK
Robert Huffaker, in his chapter entitled 'Lasting Fiction', comments, 'Fowles's third novel, *The French Lieutenant's Woman*, stands among his finer efforts. Although the book's success depends largely upon chatty Victorian narrative, its plot proceeds with wit so lively, suspense so pleasant, and observations so intelligent that the novel instructs the reader without failing to delight him' (*John Fowles*, p. 131).

Fowles engaged in correspondence with Rose, recognising the validity of the analysis.

Susan Onega, in *Form and Meaning in the Novels of John Fowles*, looks at Fowles's experimental approaches as well as considering his major existential concern, that of the freedom of the individual in relation to society. She gives two questions as the keys to open the search that Fowles undertakes in his novels, not least in *The French Lieutenant's Woman*: 'What is the meaning and purpose of human life? and What is the status of reality?' (p. 9).

Katherine Tarbox's *The Art of John Fowles* deals with various aspects of the book including narrative perspective, and the themes of time, love and the survival of individual freedom. There is also a transcript of an interview with John Fowles.

H. W. Fawkner's critique takes the idea of 'temporality' as its main theme and looks at how 'separate series of actions support each other through the confluence of time, the sheer fluidity of time'. Separate chapters on 'Evolution' and 'Emancipation' deal with these two themes in *The French Lieutenant's Woman*, as well as the other novels. Fowles approved of this critique and contributed a foreword to the book. Fawkner also contributes to the Aubrey compilation of essays an essay on nature as a central concern in Fowles's novels.

More recently, William Stephenson's *John Fowles* in the Writers and Their Work series (2003) looks at Fowles's work in three chronological periods from the points of view of literary and biographical influences. There is acknowledgement of Fowles's awareness of **poststructuralism**, but also his strong sense of the literary antecedents that contribute to the structure and the narrative style of *The French Lieutenant's Woman.*

In addition to these books, there are many articles in journals and increasingly on websites that provide further critical insights. Some of these articles, as well as new material, have been collected into volumes. James Aubrey's *John Fowles and Nature: Fourteen Perspectives on Landscape* (1999) contains several useful essays on *The French Lieutenant's Woman* by eminent Fowles critics, with

CHECK THE BOOK
Simon Loveday accounts for the 'tremendous popularity' of *The French Lieutenant's Woman*, noting that 'Fowles has combined the historical novel with the self-conscious work of fiction, thus appealing to a variety of different types of reader and creating an unusual combination of period flavour with anachronism, nostalgia with irony' (*The Romances of John Fowles*, p. 48).

landscape and nature as the unifying theme: essays with specific focus on *The French Lieutenant's Woman* include those by Patricia Beatty, H. W. Fawkner, Kevin Padian, Suzanne Ross and Eileen Warburton (author of the Fowles biography), and there is interesting background on geology and geography from the combined thoughts of Liz-Anne Bawden, Kevin Padian and Hugh S. Torrens.

Another useful collection, mentioned earlier, is *Critical Essays on John Fowles*, edited by Ellen Pifer (1986), which includes three general pieces on the unity of Fowles's fiction and Linda Hutcheon's essay 'The "Real World(s)" of Fiction: *The French Lieutenant's Woman*'.

One of the best overviews of **postmodernism** is to be found in Christian Gutleben's book *Nostalgic Postmodernism: The Victorian Tradition and the Contemporary British Novel* (2001), which makes detailed reference to *The French Lieutenant's Woman*. Gutleben considers other writers who revert to the Victorian tradition from a twentieth-century perspective.

The writings of John Fowles himself also develop ideas explored in his novels and in his approach to the art and craft of writing. Particularly useful with reference to *The French Lieutenant's Woman* are the following: 'Notes on an Unfinished Novel', 'Hardy and the Hag' and 'An Unholy Inquisition', all of which appear in *Wormholes: Essays and Occasional Writings* (1998). Following John Fowles's death in November 2007, several obituaries appeared in major newspapers, magazines and other media in this country and abroad, commenting on his achievement. Some of these are referred to in the section **John Fowles's life and works**. Others are recorded in **Further reading**.

CONTEMPORARY APPROACHES

You may find it useful to complement the approaches suggested below with references to the critical works indicated. The important thing to keep in mind is that these critical works often overlap, are not mutually exclusive and help the reader towards a personal, but informed, response.

PSYCHOLOGICAL APPROACHES

Jungian and Freudian critical approaches both suggest ways of looking at *The French Lieutenant's Woman*, the former tending to look at characters in the **narrative** and the latter tending to focus on the author/narrator with his concerns, intentions and influences. Fowles, in his correspondence and his notes on writing, has commented on the broad distinction between the two. It is possible to take ideas from both approaches, since the narrator himself appears on several occasions in the novel, either as an intrusive commentator or, equally importantly, as a character who literally walks into his own narrative.

The Jungian approach offers a cogent, unifying approach to the novel. It identifies five features from the writings of Carl Jung that can be supported by detailed reference to text. The best outline of the approach, with a thorough analysis of *The French Lieutenant's Woman*, comes from Carol M. Barnum in *The Fiction of John Fowles: A Myth for Our Time*. She identifies the three Jungian archetypes: the shadow, the anima and the mandala. She then describes how these fit into a further Jungian concept, that of the mythical quest in which the protagonist is guided by an older man towards understanding of the self – in Jungian terms, individuation. In her chapter 'The French Lieutenant's Woman: The Evolution of an Emerging Quester', Carol Barnum identifies the shadow as the hidden side of the incomplete Charles. The anima figure, the one who will lead Charles to psychological understanding, is Sarah. The mandala is described by Jung as 'individuation' or 'the wholeness of the self', the search for this wholeness of being that Charles seeks. The journey towards this sense of individuation takes on the form of a mythic journey or quest. The old man one might assume to be Dr Grogan. However, as if to prove that no one formula will suffice with *The French Lieutenant's Woman*, Fowles uses Sarah as the guide as well as the anima figure. This model offers insights into several aspects of the novel and can be well documented from the text.

Another critic who identifies a Jungian interpretation is Robert Huffaker, who in *John Fowles* (1980) sees Sarah as the anima figure

> **CONTEXT**
>
> Jung saw the unconscious in the human mind as divided into two distinct parts: the personal and the universal. It is the universal element, with its shared images or archetypes, which finds expression in art and literature and in mythologies.

(p. 109), the Jungian intuitive woman, whose 'moods and emotions do not come to her directly from the unconscious, but are peculiar to her feminine nature. They are therefore never naïve, but mixed with unacknowledged purpose' (Carl Jung, *Contributions to Analytical Research*, trans. H. G. and C. F. Baynes, 1988, p. 170).

Several other critics, including Carol M. Barnum, Barry N. Olshen, Robert Huffaker, Ronald Binns, Thomas C. Foster and Katherine Tarbox, identify the search for individual wholeness as the essential quest of the protagonists. Details of their works are given in **Further reading**.

The Freudian approach relies heavily on a sexual pattern in Charles's situation. Gilbert Rose suggests several parallels between Sarah the young prostitute and Sarah Woodruff. He notes the desertion by a lover, the period of two years' absence and the daughter. The prostitute's daughter is said to 'lall' (p. 308), babble, and we later discover that Sarah Woodruff's daughter is called Lalage. In both episodes Charles placates the child with a watch, which it is suggested may be a subconscious wish to reverse time. Rose traces the pattern in Charles's own history, 'a life with only one tragedy', which is that his mother and the daughter she was carrying had both died in childbirth. He goes on to suggest that the marriage of Charles's parents lasted a possible two-year period. Charles's quest is seen as an attempt to recover the past and replace the lost sister. This leads to an interpretation of the strange vision at the end of Chapter 20: 'a figure, a dark shadow, his dead sister, moved ahead of him, lightly, luringly, up the ashlar steps and into the broken column's mystery' (p. 173). The implication in the Freudian sense is that Charles is seeking a subconscious sexual fulfilment and that this accounts for his horror in any sexual encounters with the two women. Rose extends the idea of Freudian guilt by suggesting that Charles is seeking a union with the lost mother.

Sarah's insistence that Charles cannot marry her (p. 343) may show insight into Charles's subconscious. Charles's realisation about the 'ghostly presence of the past' (pp. 350–1) may also be explained in Freudian terms. There may be a Freudian explanation for the

CONTEXT

In an interview with Mel Gussow, Fowles said, 'When a book is reviewed, it is like the weaning of children. You're kicked about or even praised – and the book is separated from you. At a conscious level, this may be painful. But at an unconscious level this leaves one free – to write another novel' (John Fowles in 'Talk With John Fowles', Mel Gussow, *New York Times*, 13 November 1977).

inclusion of the tenuous suggestion of an incestuous relationship between Thomas Hardy and his cousin, or possibly half-sister, Tryphena Sparks.

Fowles, whose book was two years in 'gestation', was attracted to Rose's interpretations, engaged in correspondence with him and refers to his analysis as a 'plausible and attractive model' in the essay 'Hardy and the Hag' in *Wormholes*.

MARXISM AND MARXIST CRITICISM

One should distinguish at the outset between **Marxism** as it is presented in *The French Lieutenant's Woman* and Marxist critical theory. From the introduction of Marx on page 18 of the book as a contemporary of the 1867 characters, through the epigraphs to Chapters 7, 12, 30, 37 and 42 – the last of which is picked up in the penultimate paragraph of the novel – Fowles seems to be working with what David W. Landrum calls a 'meta-narrative of Marxism' ('Rewriting Marx: Emancipation and Restoration in *The French Lieutenant's Woman*' in *Twentieth Century Literature* 42:1, Spring 1996, p. 103). As such, Marxism is a part of the way in which Fowles explores the ideas of emancipation and the restoration of human relationships without it necessarily providing a total solution, as the final paragraph of the novel indicates.

Marxist critical theory, which developed in the 1930s, opens a valuable line of enquiry into a text. It is based on class differences – economic, social and political – and looks at the values that are reinforced or subverted by the text. It examines how characters from different classes interact or are seen in conflict. Thus, we can see Ernestina's pursuit of Charles, her father's offer of work to Charles, Charles's rejection of that offer and his inability to adapt, and Sam's rebellion against his master and his subsequent progress in the Freeman capitalist enterprise in Marxist critical terms.

With regard to *The French Lieutenant's Woman*, Marxism as a theory explores the way that the freedom of the individual is seen against the 'iron laws of convention' (p. 301). In Marxist terms, the two endings of the **narrative** provide contrasting interpretations of emancipation and conformity. In the first, the existentialist freedom

CHECK THE BOOK

In his essay on Thomas Hardy, Fowles provides a Freudian interpretation of Hardy's *The Well-Beloved*, a novel that has some reflections in *The French Lieutenant's Woman* (John Fowles, 'Hardy and the Hag', in *Wormholes*, pp. 146–51).

CHECK THE NET

For a compact summary of the recurrent terms in Marxist critical theory, how texts are examined and how other approaches resemble Marxist literary criticism, visit **www. assumption.edu** and enter 'Marxism' into the search box.

CONTEXT

Some editions of *The French Lieutenant's Woman* have an introductory epigraph that is referred to by critics. The Vintage edition does not include it. However, its application to the novel and to the context of some critical commentaries may be useful: 'Every emancipation is a restoration of the human world and of human relationships to man himself' (Karl Marx, *Zur Judenfrage* [*On the Jewish Question*]).

of the individual is sacrificed to the traditional values of society. In the second, the freedom of the individual is asserted, but there is no sense of human relationships continuing, at least as far as a resolution of the lives of the two protagonists is concerned.

FEMINISM

There are differences of opinion among critics as to whether *The French Lieutenant's Woman* is open to a feminist interpretation in terms of theme or character. A totally feminist approach will miss much, as equally will a response that ignores the feminist issues raised in the book.

As an approach to writing or reading a text, feminism, and subsequent developments in post-feminism and second and third wave movements, address the way that assumptions about women feature in social, political, economic, artistic and moral ways. In a broad sense, feminism has attempted to promote the rights of women in a generally patriarchal society. Taking the themes that a feminist approach suggests – patriarchy, male chauvinism, female stereotyping, the oppression of women, the treatment of women as objects – it is clear that these are, if not central to the **narrative**, then certainly major aspects.

The history of feminism can be traced back to Mary Wollstonecraft's *A Vindication of the Rights of Woman* (1792). The term 'feminism' appeared some time after this, coined by Charles Fourier in 1837, though he had argued for women's rights as early as 1808. In *The French Lieutenant's Woman* we find many **allusions** to feminist writers and issues. We are reminded in the novel that 'John Stuart Mill had seized an opportunity in one of the early debates on the Reform Bill that now was the time to give women equal rights at the ballot box'. The date is specified: 'March 30th, 1867, is the point from which we can date the beginning of feminine emancipation in England' (p. 115). Mill's *The Subjection of Women* also appeared in 1867, and Girton College, Cambridge, opened as the first residential college for women in October that year.

QUESTION

In what ways does Sarah's situation reveal the oppression of women in the mid Victorian period?

Other references that foreground feminism include the mention of Mrs Caroline Norton, 'an ardent feminist', whose poem *The Lady of La Garaye* is said to be 'a eulogy of Florence Nightingale', which was why 'the poem struck so deep in so many feminine hearts in that decade' (p. 114). One hundred years later Germaine Greer's *The Female Eunuch* (1970) was published, while in 1963 Fowles had read Betty Friedan's *The Feminine Mystique*. Eileen Warburton notes that 'the myth-drenched character of Sarah Woodruff appeared in 1969, a watershed moment in the American feminist movement' (*John Fowles: A Life in Two Worlds*, p. 317).

Fowles has stated: 'I have for many years worked in predominantly female environments and I am a feminist – that is I like women and enjoy their company' ('I Write Therefore I Am' (1964), in *Wormholes*, p. 8).

There is a slight **ambiguity** in Fowles's definition, and maybe this male-oriented treatment of feminism accounts for some of the contrasting readings of feminism in the novel. Sarah's feminism is clear in the words she uses, notably in her 'credo' on page 430; she creates her own fictions, notably in her account to Charles in Chapter 20, in order to reject Victorian patriarchal values. Charles, too, perceives her as possessing an 'independence of spirit' and the narrator sees an implicit modernity in her whereby 'we can sometimes see the looks of a century ago on a modern face: but never those of a century to come' (p. 176). In her final appearance in Chapter 60, in 'the full uniform of the New Woman, flagrantly rejecting all formal contemporary notions of female fashion', she is seen by Charles as 'the remarkable creature of his happier memories – but blossomed, realized, winged from the black pupa'. Magali Cornier Michael questions Charles's support of feminism in that 'throughout most of the novel Charles is portrayed as chauvinistic and unable to step outside of his masculine perspective' ('"Who is Sarah?": A Critique of *The French Lieutenant's Woman*'s Feminism' in *Critique: Studies in Modern Fiction*, Vol. 28, No. 4, Summer 1987). This balance between Fowles's assertion of feminism, the clearly foregrounded feminist issues in the novel, Charles's ambiguous support of feminism and Sarah's own voice lies at the heart of any feminist approach. For this reason, such an approach can provide many insights into character and theme.

CHECK THE BOOK

'The actions of Sarah that are reported do suggest that she is a woman who rebels against patriarchal society by casting herself outside that society and thus outside masculine ideology. The problem, however, is that the Sarah who performs these revolutionary acts has no existence outside of the male perspectives that depict her' (Magali Cornier Michael, 'Who is Sarah?').

FEMINISM continued

CHECK THE BOOK

In an interview with Carol Barnum, Fowles, speaking of Sarah, says: 'I deliberately left her character and motivations open, and I am not going to encourage one interpretation over another' ('An Interview with John Fowles' in *Modern Fiction Studies* 31, Spring 1985, pp. 195–6).

A relatively modern extension of feminism is eco-feminism, which offers further insights into *The French Lieutenant's Woman* from the perspective of masculine subordination of women and the environment. The term was coined in 1974 by Françoise d'Eaubonne, and James Aubrey's edited collection of essays, *John Fowles and Nature*, contains useful interpretations from Suzanne Ross, Eileen Warburton and Carol Barnum that acknowledge Fowles's assertion in *The Tree* that nature is the key to his fiction. See **Themes: Nature** and **Narrative techniques and language** for the portrayel of nature in the novel.

PART FIVE

BACKGROUND

JOHN FOWLES'S LIFE AND WORKS

John (Robert) Fowles (1926–2005) was born in Leigh-on-Sea, Essex, the son of a wealthy cigar merchant. Fowles has claimed that the respectability of his life in his home town with its oppressive and conformist attitudes had a 'depressive effect' on him.

He was educated first at Alleyn Court School and then for four years at Bedford School, where he became Captain of Prefects, a sort of head boy with the power of corporal punishment over the younger boys, a practice that Fowles carried out but despised as a 'terrible system'.

During the Second World War the family moved to a small village in Devon close to Dartmoor. Here Fowles's love of nature developed into what was to be a lifelong fascination. Many passages in his novels reveal his knowledge and love of natural history.

In 1944 Fowles went to Edinburgh University as part of his military training and from 1945 to 1946 he completed his National Service in the Royal Marines. He ultimately rejected a career in the Marines and took up a place at New College Oxford, where he graduated in 1950 with a degree in French and German. It was during this time that Fowles took an interest in French Existentialism, particularly the writings of Camus and Sartre.

Fowles worked for one year in France as a teacher/lecturer at the University of Poitiers, after which he spent two years as a teacher at a boys' school on the island of Spetses in Greece. It was during this period that Fowles began to work on writing projects, including drafts of *The Magus*, though he did not submit any manuscripts for publication at the time, considering them unsatisfactory, incomplete or too lengthy. During his stay in Greece he met his wife Elizabeth Whitton, who was already married to a teacher at the school and had a daughter. Elizabeth went through a difficult divorce, and she

> **CONTEXT**
>
> In an obituary, Sarah Lyall comments that 'in an autobiographical essay, he [Fowles] describes his hometown as a place "dominated by conformism – the pursuit of respectability". Although, to all appearances, he thrived in the environment – "I was given some facility with masks" was how he put it – his early years left him with a distaste for following the herd' ('John Fowles, British Author of Ambiguous Endings, Dies at 79', obituary *New York Times*, 7 November 2005).

CONTEXT

In an interview with Dianne Vipond, John Fowles commented: 'I've often said that I've written about only one woman in my life. I often feel when writing that the heroine of one novel is the same woman as the heroine of another ... In my own life that one woman has been my wife, Elizabeth, who died in 1990. I've thought about trying to do an account of her but so far haven't, knowing she lies so close behind many of my characters' ('An Unholy Inquisition', *Wormholes*, p. 380).

and Fowles eventually married in 1956. Elizabeth helped Fowles with suggestions on the early novels, though later her influence on him diminished. However, as he openly declared, she was the inspiration behind many of his female characters.

On his return to England Fowles continued to teach, first at Ashridge College for one year and then from 1954 to 1963 at St Godric's College, where he became a Head of Department. In the 1960s the first draft of *The Collector* was completed in a matter of some four weeks. After revision, it was submitted for publication. It tells the story of a butterfly collector, who purchases with his football pools winnings a secluded mansion house with a cellar, in which he imprisons a young woman. The themes of control and freedom are reflected in **allusions** to Shakespeare's *The Tempest* – the young woman is called Miranda and she refers to her captor, Freddie Clegg, as 'Caliban'. She dies without gaining her freedom, and the novel ends on a chilling note as Clegg contemplates a second victim. The novel came out in 1963, its immediate success in terms of critical reception and sales enabling Fowles to leave his teaching post and concentrate on writing.

A collection of short philosophical pieces appeared in 1964 in *The Aristos*, influenced by the French idea of *pensées* – the thoughts of the author on sigificant topics. In 1965 the revised manuscripts of *The Magus* were submitted to the publisher. This novel has clear parallels again with *The Tempest* and also with Homer's *The Odyssey*. With its mysterious, romantic, psychoanalytical, complex, mythological, at times surreal qualities, it became something of a cult novel, particularly in the United States. The original title had been *The Godgame*, taken from the God-like control that the millionaire Conchis exerts over Nicholas Urfe, a teacher at a boys' school on the Greek island of Phraxos. Fowles revised the book over several years, and in 1977 the novel was re-issued with a changed, more **ambiguous** ending.

It was in 1966 that Fowles moved to Lyme Regis, to Underhill Farm on the cliffs overlooking the sea. This became the setting for the Dairy in *The French Lieutenant's Woman*. After a landslip he moved to Belmont House, higher above Lyme Bay, and this was to be his home for the rest of his life. It provided him with the isolated existence he sought, as well as the setting for *The French Lieutenant's Woman* and a series of small texts on the history of the town and collections of photographs of the area. In 1978 he became honorary curator of the Lyme Regis Museum and served in this position until a stroke in 1988 caused him to retire.

The 1969 publication of *The French Lieutenant's Woman* brought Fowles both critical acclaim and financial reward. It was in the late sixties that Anna Christy, Elizabeth's daughter from her first marriage, re-established a relationship with her mother and John Fowles. It was suggested by Eileen Warburton that this reconciliation contributed to the mother–daughter echoes in *The French Lieutenant's Woman* (*John Fowles: A Life in Two Worlds*, 2004).

A collection of short stories, the *Ebony Tower: Collected Novellas*, appeared in 1974. The first title suggested was *Variations*, since there seems to be a unifying theme of failure or dissatisfaction in spite of apparent success.

Daniel Martin, the search into the past for identity by an English screenwriter, appeared in 1977. Fowles described the novel as being about 'Englishness', and the **narrative**, with a Hardyesque love triangle, is complemented by **allusions** to and observations on philosophy, culture, archaeology and myth, with some thoughts about the difference between British and American culture, and also the different art forms of literature and the cinema.

In 1981 the dilemma of how to transpose a complex, multi-layered novel onto the film screen was resolved in the release of *The French Lieutenant's Woman*, which was to be the most successful adaptation of any of Fowles's novels. The film, starring Meryl Streep and Jeremy Irons, was directed by Karel Reisz with screenplay by the dramatist Harold Pinter, and gave Fowles's work further popularity.

Between *Daniel Martin* and the publication of *A Maggot*, Fowles worked on several projects, including the text for collections of photographs, the histories of Lyme, French translations and

CHECK THE BOOK

'The mysteriously suffering Sarah Woodruff dramatized Elizabeth's guilt, isolation, and obliterating entrapment, as well as her intuitive longing for something better. Several key scenes in the novel are also emotionally supercharged by the mother–daughter reunion of Liz and Anna in 1966' (Warburton, *John Fowles*, p. 293).

adaptations, and editing books such as *Monumenta Britannica* and *Thomas Hardy's England*. *Mantissa* appeared in 1982, a novel in which the female character is less central to the action. Warburton, in the biography, suggests that after *The French Lieutenant's Woman* Fowles's more distant literary relationship with Elizabeth, who had previously contributed much to the editing, changed the style of writing (*John Fowles: A Life in Two Worlds*, p. 330).

In 1985 Fowles published *A Maggot*, a murder mystery set in early eighteenth-century Devon. The disappearance of two of a group of five travellers is investigated. The testimonies of the other three in the group reveal a mysterious encounter with visitors from the future. The novel, like *The Magus*, is complex and multi-layered in its different time perspectives.

John Fowles suffered a stroke in 1988 that affected his right side and impeded his writing, though he did recover and was able to complete some shorter writing projects. Two years later, in 1990, the death of Elizabeth affected Fowles badly. Later that year, however, he began a relationship with a young Oxford student who had called at Belmont House. The affair with Elena van Lieshout lasted for two years, coming to an end in November 1992. From 1993 to 1997 Fowles's companion was Anna Peebles, a painter and art teacher.

In 1990 John Fowles's archives were purchased by the Harry Ransom Humanties Research Center at the University of Texas in Austin, though the documents would remain at the University of Exeter while Fowles worked on them for the edited versions that appeared eventually in the two volumes of *Journals*.

Fowles's last essay, 'The Nature of Nature', was published in 1996. That year also saw a significant event in Lyme, the John Fowles Symposium, organised by the Lyme Regis Philpot Museum. Entitled 'John Fowles: Love, Loss and Landscape', it was attended by sixty scholars and included a guided walk through the Undercliff. James Aubrey, Professor of English in Denver, Colorado, helped with the organisation.

In 1977 a collection of essays and occasional writings was prepared and edited with the assistance of Jan Relf, an academic friend. In 1998 this collection appeared under the title *Wormholes*. It is made up of thirty pieces of writing covering the major part of Fowles's writing career and reveals much about his preoccupations and views during this period. Several other shorter pieces of work were published in subsequent years, and Fowles also worked on a number of translations and adaptations from the French.

Fowles was also interested in conservation and concerned about the effects of pollution on the south coast. This stemmed from his life-long love of natural history and is reflected in his non-fiction as well as in the detailed observations of the natural world in his novels, not least in *The French Lieutenant's Woman*.

In 1998 Fowles married Sarah Smith, who was to remain with him until his death. Fowles had gained a reputation as a rather remote character, a fact that he wryly acknowledged in a 2003 interview for *The Guardian*: 'I know I have a reputation as a cantankerous man of letters and I don't try and play it down.' That this persona was probably unjustified is confirmed by the many who interviewed him. His second wife, Sarah Fowles, said: 'He was a very, very private man. He had a warm and lovely public persona but underneath was very shy' (quoted by Charlotte Higgins, 'Quiet Passing for author John Fowles', in *The Guardian*, 9 November 2005).

Fowles's great passion was a love of language. The BBC News obituary says that 'even Fowles could be impressed by the discovery of rare treasure in his writing. He said, "Occasionally you're lucky and you hit on something deeper. And that is really marvellous"' (story from BBC News, 11 July 2005).

Before his death, two volumes of *John Fowles: The Journals* were published. Along with the Eileen Warburton biography of Fowles, *John Fowles: A Life in Two Worlds*, which appeared in 2004, they provide valuable insights into the complexities of the man and the writer. Fowles's contributions to literature were acknowledged in awards (Silver Pen Award 1969, W. H. Smith Literary Award 1970,

CHECK THE BOOK

A tribute to John Fowles's writings on the natural world is made by James Aubrey in his introduction to *John Fowles and Nature*, a collection of fourteen essays: 'Another feature of Fowles's writing that should make him a spokesman for the age is the call to awareness of the natural world that has long informed his writing' (p. 13).

CHECK THE BOOK

The *Journals* provide a comprehensive insight into Fowles's life to almost the last years. The second volume will be of greater interest to the student of *The French Lieutenant's Woman*, with its many references to the novel and the subsequent film (see *John Fowles: The Journals*, Vols 1 and 2, ed. Charles Drazin, 2003 and 2006).

Christopher Award 1981) and a nomination in 1999 for the Nobel Prize in Literature. Fowles was also made an Honorary Fellow of New College Oxford (1997) and received honorary doctorates in literature from the University of East Anglia (1997) and Exeter University (1983).

John Fowles's death on 5 November 2005 in Axminster Hospital near Lyme Regis was recorded in obituaries in all major newspapers and journals in Britain and the United States, as well as in other parts of the world. His agent Anthony Shiel said: 'He was a literary writer who always had a reader in mind and wanted to communicate.' Melvyn Bragg, the novelist and television presenter, added this telling comment: 'Literary talk about which books will last and for how long is mostly no more than a pleasant or rather malicious way of passing the time, but I'll be surprised if *The French Lieutenant's Woman* did not float down the stream for some decades, while his work in Lyme Regis could run for generations' ('John Fowles will be missed' in *The Guardian*, Tuesday, 8 November 2005).

CHECK THE NET

For a selection of obituary tributes to John Fowles, try the following: **www. fowlesbooks.com/ Appreciation. html**. This site will direct you to three other obituaries from the BBC, *The Guardian* and *The Telegraph*.

HISTORICAL BACKGROUND

It is necessary to provide two historical backgrounds for a novel written in the 1960s about events taking place in the 1860s. However, the two are interwoven into a compelling single **narrative**, a nineteenth-century story with a twentieth-century narrative perspective. There are many overt references and more subtle **allusions** to people and events of the Victorian age in the fabric of the narrative itself. Many of these are included in this brief survey of the features that shaped the age that Charles Smithson was living in and moving towards.

Britain in the 1860s had emerged virtually unscathed from the political revolutions that swept across Europe in 1848. Though social change was approaching, Britain enjoyed a relatively peaceful and prosperous time. The results of what may be termed 'the first industrial revolution' of the latter half of the eighteenth and the first half of the nineteenth century had produced changes that were celebrated in the Great Exhibition of 1851. The stability of this mid Victorian age would, however, soon be altered by developments in the economic, commercial, political, industrial, scientific and social fields that would determine the nature of the second half of the nineteenth century and the beginnings of the twentieth. It has been suggested that the twentieth century began in the 1860s.

On page 18 of the book we are told of Karl Marx working on *Das Kapital*, the first of three influential political and economic studies (the latter two completed from Marx's notes by Friedrich Engels). Marxist theory analyses history in terms of class conflict and predicts many of the changes that are shown to be evolving in *The French Lieutenant's Woman*. There was political and social conflict of a similar nature in the struggle between the Liberal and Conservative parties over the final Reform Bill of 1867 that would lead to the emancipation of the working classes by their obtaining voting rights. Economic factors also led to the rise of an increasingly influential middle class with energy and ambition, which contrasted with the leisured upper classes with their belief in the continuance of secure social stratification and order.

On the broader political scene, the emergence of the United States of America, working through its period of Reconstruction after the American Civil War, is instrumental in Charles Smithson's perceiving new possibilities of freedom in 1869.

Darwin's *On the Origin of Species* (1859), which led to the development of the theory of evolution by natural selection and the concept of 'the survival of the fittest', would shake the religious foundations of the Victorian age in its challenge to the biblical account of creation. Charles Lyell's work on geology in the 1830s had opened up a vast timescale that altered views about man's place in history and added to the force of Darwinian evolutionary theory.

Other movements of an entirely different kind would also trouble the establishment, in particular the church. The Oxford Movement sought a return to the rituals and ornamentation that the Reformation had abolished, and this contributed to a demand for

---

CONTEXT

'Marx's laboratory for working out his ideas of class was Britain, where, according to his formulation, the Industrial Revolution was in the throes of creating the world's first authentic proletariat, defined by mechanised, factory and, above all, waged labour; by starker contrast between owners and producers than had existed before; by social discord; and by deep-seated antagonism across class lines' (Jeremy Black and Donald M. MacRaild, *Nineteenth-Century Britain*, 2003, p. 105).

 CHECK THE NET

The concept of geologic history is referred to as 'deep time'. For a well-illustrated site that explains the concept, visit **www.pbs.org** and enter 'Deep time' into the search box.

Roman Catholic emancipation. Dissenting traditions, notably the different forms of Methodism that were often popular with the successful industrial and commercial classes, also challenged Anglicanism.

CHECK THE NET

For a website offering links to Mill, Bentham and several other utilitarian connections, visit **www. utiltarianism.com**

The works of John Stuart Mill and Jeremy Bentham challenged traditional Victorian values in their promotion of utilitarianism, whose central doctrine was that the happiness of man was the only measure of right and wrong. Mill's work *The Subjection of Women*, which appeared in 1869, was based on utilitarian principles and advocated the rights of women in society. Victorian society and attitudes were largely male-dominated. The emergence of women unwilling to accept the stifling roles dictated by a patriarchal society would characterise the latter part of the nineteenth century, lead to the idea of the New Woman and continue well into the twentieth century.

The emergence of the Pre-Raphaelite Brotherhood later in the nineteenth century becomes an important element in the **narrative**, providing Sarah Woodruff with a milieu in which she feels she has found a kind of individual independence, a situation that is foreshadowed by a number of images earlier in the narrative.

This is the historical framework within which the lives of the characters are played out. It is also the framework within which Fowles, from his perspective of one hundred years later, operates.

The 1960s were similar to the 1860s in the sense that vast changes were taking place that would shape the rest of the century. Many of the events of Fowles's time mirrored events in the 1860s. John Fowles lived in a period that saw the threat of nuclear war, coming to a head in the Cuban missile confrontation between Russia and America and shaking the whole world as much as Darwinism had the Victorians. The passing of the Civil Rights Act in America, a hundred years after Reconstruction, had not been without its troubles and the subsequent assassinations of key figures in human rights – John Kennedy, his brother Robert and Martin Luther King – had reverberations far beyond America's shores. In Britain immigration restrictions were placed on British subjects from the

CONTEXT

If any one record album can catch the spirit of the age in the late 1960s in terms of popular culture, it must be the Beatles' *Sergeant Pepper's Lonely Hearts Club Band*. Released on 1 June 1967, it was acknowledged by major critics in the music industry as the most influential album of all time.

Commonwealth, though an emergent multicultural society was gradually altering many facets of traditional British life.

Marxist ideologies had been distorted and led to the term 'the Iron Curtain', which would culminate in the building of the Berlin Wall in 1961. Space travel, as radical a concept as the railway had been to the nineteenth century, was a reality and in 1969 the first man walked on the surface of the moon. The feminist movement, begun in the nineteenth century, was still active in the twentieth, with the Women's Liberation movement, the availability of the contraceptive pill and the legalisation of abortion. Changes in the homosexuality laws and the dismissal of charges of obscenity against Penguin Books' publication of D. H. Lawrence's *Lady Chatterley's Lover* in 1963 were signs of a new freedom in sexual attitudes. Class boundaries, still a peculiarly British phenomenon, were being challenged by a number of developments in popular and particularly youth culture, though many still longed for a return to Victorian values, whatever they were perceived to have been.

Darwinism and the theory of evolution was still in the news in 1967 and the following were all significant events: the trial and guilty verdict in Tennessee of John Scopes for teaching evolution; publication of Desmond Morris's *The Naked Ape*; palaeontologist Louis Leakey finding pre-human fossils in Kenya that extended the theory and understanding of evolution.

LITERARY BACKGROUND

The mid Victorian era was a high point in the development of the novel. Besides the major names – Austen, the Brontës, Collins, Dickens, Eliot, Mrs Gaskell, Scott, Trollope, Thackeray – a host of other writers, many of whose names and works are long out of fashion, were producing literature for a growing reading public. Significant in *The French Lieutenant's Woman* and in Fowles's own life in Dorset is the influence of Thomas Hardy, not only as a novelist but also as a poet. Poetry produced other important figures whose work was influential in shaping the cultural and also the

CONTEXT

An example of how Victorian poetry reinforced social values and attitudes is found in these lines from Tennyson: 'Man for the field and woman for the hearth; / Man for the sword, and for the needle she; / Man with the head, and women with the heart; / Man to command, and woman to obey; / All else is confusion' (Alfred Lord Tennyson, *The Princess*, 1847).

CHECK THE NET

For a comprehensive website with numerous informative links celebrating the 200th anniversary of Charles Darwin's birthday on 12 February 2009, visit **www. darwin200.org**

CHECK THE BOOK

A recent excellent addition to neo-Victorian literature (see below) is the multi-faceted study *The Suspicions of Mr Whicher* by Kate Summerscale (2008), a detective story combining historical research, biographical detail, and literary and sociological comment.

CHECK THE BOOK

Malcolm Bradbury, the novelist and critic, says: 'The French Lieutenant's Woman seems to me one of the best books that have come out of Britain since the war, and I think it very self-conscious. It appeared at a time when many British writers were rethinking their relationship to their tradition' ('The Novelist as Impressario', in *No, Not Bloomsbury*, 1987, p. 282).

social environment. Extracts from the poetry of Hardy, Alfred Lord Tennyson, A. H. Clough and Matthew Arnold all feature in the text and epigraphs of *The French Lieutenant's Woman*.

The latter part of *The French Lieutenant's Woman* has elements of detective and sensational fiction. The popularity of the genre in the Victorian era was not confined to Arthur Conan Doyle's well-known adventures of Sherlock Holmes, which did not appear until 1891. Wilkie Collins, with *The Woman in White* (1860) and *The Moonstone* (1868), was an early exponent of the genre, while Dickens's *Bleak House* (1852) introduced the first detective in British fiction. Charles's search for the missing Sarah and his employment of private detective agencies imitates the genre in a further dimension of the **pastiche/parody** features.

In the 1960s, in terms of the novel in general and *The French Lieutenant's Woman* in particular, Fowles found himself in a strange position with regard to tradition and the avant-garde. The narrator of *The French Lieutenant's Woman* looks to the past and imitates the great Victorian novelists, yet acknowledges that he belongs to the age of Alain Robbe-Grillet and Roland Barthes, proponents of the *nouveau roman*.

Traditional elements of the novel are seen in the romantic storyline, the pressures of a restrictive class system, an omniscient narrative voice and a strong, independent woman seeking her fulfilment in a society that denies her opportunity. At the same time, the narrator regularly intrudes into his own **narrative**, refuses to provide a neat Victorian ending to the story and, in fact, provides two, possibly three, alternatives, thereby drawing the reader into complicity with a manipulative narrator.

The narrative also acknowledges the emergence of existentialism, psychoanalytic theory and **modernism**, ideas that developed in the intervening years between 1867 and 1967. We see endings that resemble the Victorian tradition and modernist endings similar to those of James Joyce and D. H. Lawrence, but it is in their juxtaposition within the one novel and the invitation to the reader to enter into the debate that Fowles breaks new **postmodernist** ground. William Palmer sees *The French Lieutenant's Woman* in much the same position as Charles, at a kind of crossroads, 'in suspension between two worlds' (*The Fiction of John Fowles*, p. 28).

The legacy of *The French Lieutenant's Woman* is seen in the genre that has been termed the neo-Victorian or the retro-Victorian novel. Christian Gutleben, speaking of the influence of *The French Lieutenant's Woman* in the 1960s, says, 'At its birth ... the retro-Victorian novel and its ironic recycling of the myth-laden Victorian novel was at the avant-garde of postmodernism in Britain' (*Nostalgic Postmodernism*, 2001, p. 120). Certainly, since 1967 there has been a growing interest in recreating and reshaping the Victorian novel, in terms of either pastiche or parody.

CHECK THE BOOK

Neo-Victorian texts include A. S. Byatt's *Possession* (1990), and *Affinity* (1999) and *Fingersmith* (2002) by Sarah Waters. Christian Gutleben's *Nostalgic Postmodernism* offers a study of a wide range of major novelists up to 2000 in the neo-Victorian tradition.

World events

1837 Victoria becomes Queen

1838 Anti-Corn Law League established; National Gallery, London, opens

1841 Robert Peel becomes prime minister

1848 Revolutions in Italian and Austrian cities

1850 Re-establishmemnt of Roman Catholic hierarchy in Britain

1851 The Great Exhibition

1854 Crimean War

1857 Divorce permissible without special Act of Parliament

1858 Linnaean Society; Darwin proposes Theory of Evolution

John Fowles's life

Literary events

1838 Charles Lyell, *Elements of Geology*

1841 London Library opens; *Punch* magazine appears

1847 Emily Brontë, *Wuthering Heights*; Charlotte Brontë, *Jane Eyre*; W. M. Thackeray, *Vanity Fair*

1848 Pre-Raphaelite Brotherhood formed; Elizabeth Gaskell, *Mary Barton*; J. S. Mill, *Principles of Political Economics*; Karl Marx and Friedrich Engels, *The Communist Manifesto*

1849 Charles Dickens, *David Copperfield*

1850 Alfred, Lord Tennyson, *In Memoriam*; William Wordsworth, *The Prelude*

1851 Harriet Taylor Mill, *The Enfranchisement of Women*

1853 Charlotte Brontë, *Villette*; Dickens, *Bleak House*

1854 Dickens, *Hard Times*

1857 George Eliot, *Scenes of Clerical Life*

World events	John Fowles's life	Literary events
		1859 Eliot, *Adam Bede*; Dickens, *A Tale of Two Cities*
		1861 Dickens, *Great Expectations*
1865 Andrew Johnson President of USA		
1866 Women's Suffragette petition to Parliament		
1867 Gladstone leader of Liberal Party		**1867** Matthew Arnold, *Dover Beach*
1868 Disraeli Conservative prime minister, then Gladstone 1868–74 Liberal PM; London University admits women		**1868** Wilkie Collins, *The Moonstone*
1869 Single property-owning women vote in municipal elections; first women medical students at Edinburgh University but not allowed complete course; Ulysses S. Grant President of USA		**1869** J. S. Mill, *The Subjection of Women*; Thomas Huxley coins term 'agnostic'; Arnold, *Culture and Anarchy*
1870 Elementary Education Act; Married Women's Property Act		**1870** Death of Dickens
1871 University Religious Tests for graduation ended; Women's Education Union		**1871** Charles Darwin, *The Descent of Man*; George Eliot, *Middlemarch*
		1873 Thomas Hardy, *A Pair of Blue Eyes*
1874 Disraeli prime minister (to 1880); London Medical College for Women		**1874** Hardy, *Far from the Madding Crowd*
1878 Women admitted to Oxford; University of London degrees for women		**1878** Hardy, *The Return of the Native*
1880 Gladstone Liberal prime minister (to 1885)		

World events	John Fowles's life	Literary events
1881 Women Honours Examination at Cambridge		
1882 Married Women's Property Act		
		1883 Robert Louis Stevenson, *Treasure Island*
		1886 Hardy, *The Mayor of Casterbridge*
1891 Shopworkers' Union admits men and women equally		**1891** Hardy, *Tess of the d'Urbervilles*; George Gissing, *New Grub Street*
1894 Local Government Act – local franchise for married women		
		1895 Oscar Wilde imprisoned for homosexuality; Hardy, *Jude the Obscure*; H. G. Wells, *The Time Machine*
1897 Queen Victoria's Diamond Jubilee		**1897** Bram Stoker, *Dracula*
1899–1902 Boer War		
		1900 Joseph Conrad, *Lord Jim*
1901 Death of Queen Victoria; Edward VII becomes King		**1901** Rudyard Kipling, *Kim*
		1902 Conrad, *Heart of Darkness*
1910 Death of King Edward VII; George V becomes king		**1910** E. M. Forster, *Howard's End*
		1911 D. H. Lawrence, *The White Peacock*
1912 *Titanic* sinks		

World events	John Fowles's life	Literary events
		1913 Alain-Fournier, *Le Grand Meaulnes*; Lawrence, *Sons and Lovers*; Marcel Proust, *Du cote de chez Swann* (first part of *A la Recherche du temps perdu*)
1914–18 First World War		**1916** James Joyce, *Portrait of the Artist as a Young Man*
		1918 Lytton Strachey, *Eminent Victorians*; Luigi Pirandello, *Six Characters in Search of an Author*
		1920 Wilfred Owen, *Collected Poems*
		1922 T. S. Eliot, *The Waste Land*; Joyce, *Ulysses*
	1926 Born in Leigh-on-Sea	
		1927 Proust, *Le Temps Retrouve*; Virginia Woolf, *To the Lighthouse*
1928 Women in UK gain equal voting rights		**1928** Lawrence, *Lady Chatterley's Lover*
		1929 Ernest Hemingway, *A Farewell to Arms*; Woolf, *A Room of One's Own*
1930s The Depression years		
		1932 Aldous Huxley, *Brave New World*
	1934 Attends Alleyn Court School	
		1938 Graham Greene, *Brighton Rock*
1939 Germany invades Poland		**1939** Joyce, *Finnegan's Wake*

World events

1939–45 Second World War

1951 Festival of Britain

1953 Coronation of Queen Elizabeth II

1962 Cuban Missile Crisis

John Fowles's life

1939–40 Family moves to Ipplepen, Devon

1940–4 Bedford School

1941 First writings, a nature journal

1944 Edinburgh University as part of army training

1945–6 Served in Royal Marines

1946–50 New College Oxford

1950–1 Teacher at University of Poitiers, France

1951–2 Teacher at Anargyrios College, Spetses, Greece

1953–63 Teacher in London, first at Ashridge College, then at St Godric's College, Hampstead

1957 Marries Elizabeth Christy

Literary events

1942 Albert Camus, *The Outsider*

1944 T. S. Eliot, *Four Quartets*; J.-P. Sartre, *Huis Clos* (drama)

1945 George Orwell, *Animal Farm*; Evelyn Waugh, *Brideshead Revisited*

1949 Orwell, *Nineteen Eighty-four*

1951 J. D. Salinger, *The Catcher in the Rye*

1953 L. P. Hartley, *The Go-Between*; Arthur Miller, *The Crucible* (drama)

1954 William Golding, *Lord of the Flies*; Kingsley Amis, *Lucky Jim*

1960 Obscenity trial for publication of Lawrence's *Lady Chatterley's Lover*

1962 Anthony Burgess, *A Clockwork Orange*

World events

1963 Assassination of John F. Kennedy; Lyndon B. Johnson President of USA

1965 Comprehensive system in education initiated

1968 Assassinations of Robert Kennedy and Martin Luther King

1969 First moon landing; Concorde's first flight; Richard Nixon President of USA

1970 Edward Heath becomes prime minister

1971 Women's Liberation March in London

1972 Miners' strike

1974 Miners' strike; Harold Wilson becomes prime minister; Gerald Ford President of USA

1977 Jimmy Carter President of USA

1978–9 'Winter of Discontent' strikes

John Fowles's life

1963 First novel, *The Collector*; Cheltenham Literary Festival – first public appearance; leaves teaching

1964 *The Aristos: A Self-Portrait in Ideas*

1965 *The Magus*; moves into Underhill Farm

1966 Reunion with Anna Christy

1967 Filming of *The Magus*

1968 Screenplay for film *The Magus*; landslip at Underhill Farm; moves into Belmont House

1969 *The French Lieutenant's Woman*; Silver Pen Award

1970 W. H. Smith Literary Award

1973 *Poems*

1974 *Shipwreck*; *The Ebony Tower* (short stories)

1977 *Daniel Martin*; revises *The Magus*

1978 *Islands*; editor *Steep Holm: A Case History in the Study of Evolution*

Literary events

1964 Philip Larkin, *The Whitsun Weddings*

1965 Sylvia Plath, *Ariel*

1966 Jean Rhys, *Wide Sargasso Sea*

1968 Doris Lessing, *The Golden Notebook*

1969 Booker Prize initiated

1970 Germaine Greer, *The Female Eunuch*

1973 J. G. Farrell, *The Siege of Krishnapur*

1975 Malcolm Bradbury, *The History Man*

1978 Ian McEwan, *The Cement Garden*

World events

1979 Margaret Thatcher becomes prime minister

1982 Falklands War

1984 Violent clashes between miners and police

1989 Fall of Berlin Wall; World Wide Web invented; George Bush president of USA

1990 'Poll-tax' riots

1991 Gulf War

1992 Bill Clinton elected President of USA

John Fowles's life

1979 *Conditional* (poems); *The Tree*

1980 *The Enigma of Stonehenge*

1981 *A Brief History of Lyme*; Christopher award; film, *The French Lieutenant's Woman*

1981–2 Editor with Rodney Legg, *Monumenta Brittanica*

1982 *Mantissa*

1983 *A Short History of Lyme*; D.Litt Exeter University

1984 Editor, *Thomas Hardy's England*

1985 *A Maggot*

1988 Suffers stroke

1990 Death of Elizabeth Fowles

Literary events

1980 Umberto Eco, *The Name of the Rose*

1981 Salman Rushdie, *Midnight's Children*; A. N. Wilson, *Who Was Oswald Fish?*

1982 Thomas Keneally, *Schindler's Ark*; Peter Ackroyd, *The Great Fire of London*

1983 Alice Walker, *The Color Purple*; Graham Swift, *Waterland*

1984 Julian Barnes, *Flaubert's Parrot*; Angela Carter, *Nights at the Circus*

1985 Jeanette Winterson, *Oranges Are Not the Only Fruit*

1987 Margaret Atwood, *The Handmaid's Tale*

1988 Rushdie, *The Satanic Verses*

1989 Kazuo Ishiguro, *The Remains of the Day*

1990 Martin Amis, *London Fields*; A. S. Byatt, *Possession*

1991 Carter, *Wise Children*; Ben Okri, *The Famished Road*

1992 Michael Ondaatje, *The English Patient*

World events	John Fowles's life	Literary events
		1993 Vikram Seth, *A Suitable Boy*
		1995 Pat Barker, *The Ghost Road* (final part of *Regeneration* trilogy)
1996 Bill Clinton re-elected President of USA	**1996** John Fowles special edition *Twentieth Century Journal*; last essay, *The Nature of Nature*; American lecture tour; John Fowles Symposium at Lyme Regis	**1996** Atwood, *Alias Grace*; Swift, *Last Orders*
1997 Death of Diana, Princess of Wales; Labour wins election, with Tony Blair as prime minister	**1997** Honorary Fellow, New College Oxford; D.Litt, University of East Anglia	**1997** Bernard MacLaverty, *Grace Notes*; Mick Jackson, *The Underground Man*
	1998 *Wormholes: Essays and Occasional Writing*; marries Sarah Smith	**1998** McEwan, *Amsterdam*
		1999 Sarah Waters, *Affinity*
2001 George W. Bush becomes President of USA; attack on Twin Towers, New York		**2001** Peter Carey, *The True History of the Kelly Gang*
2003 Invasion of Iraq	**2003** *Journals*, Vol. 1	
	2004 Fowles biography by Eileen Warburton	**2004** Sarah Hall, *The Electric Michelangelo*
2005 London bomb attacks		**2005** John Banville, *The Sea*
2006 Tiktaalik fossil found	**2006** *Journals*, Vol. 2	**2006** Kiran Desai, *The Inheritance of Loss*
	2007 Dies 5 November in Axminster Hospital	**2007** Anne Enright, *The Gathering*

CRITICISM AND BACKGROUND READING

SOCIAL HISTORICAL

Geoffrey Best, *Mid-Victorian Britain 1851–75*, Weidenfield and Nicholson, 1971
> Examines the lives of people in Victorian Britain against a background of social and economic change

Phyllis Deane, *The First Industrial Revolution*, Cambridge University Press, 1976 (reprint)
> Background coverage of the revolutions in agriculture, commerce, industry and transport, as well as consideration of labour, capital and economic patterns

David McLellan, ed., *Karl Marx, Selected Writings*, Oxford, 2000
> Comprehensive overview with chronological extracts from Marx's works, editor's commentary and bibliographical details

Henry Mayhew, *London Labour and the London Poor*, 1851
> For modern editions, see *London Street Life, Selections from the Writings of Henry Mayhew*, ed. Raymond O'Malley, Chatto and Windus Educational, 1966, and *Mayhew's Characters*, ed. Peter Quennell, Spring Books, 1951

E. Royston Pike, ed., *Human Documents of the Victorian Golden Age*, George Allen and Unwin, 1967
> Primary sources for historical, social and political background

Jerry White, *London in the Nineteenth Century*, Vintage, 2008
> Full coverage of the city and its people, culture, work, law and order in the nineteenth century

A. N. Wilson, *The Victorians*, Arrow, 2003
> An evocative portrait of the age with historical detail and amusing anecdotes; recommended as an introduction to and overview of the age

LITERATURE BACKGROUND

James Acheson, ed., *The British and Irish Novel since 1960*, St Martin's Press, 1991
> A collection of essays on major novelists, including 'John Fowles and the Fiction of Freedom' by Lance St John Butler

Steven Connor, *The English Novel in History 1950–1995*, Routledge, 1996
> A wide-ranging study of post-war fiction, covering the major influential writers in relation to the development of the novel, the media and the reading public

Christian Gutleben, *Nostalgic Postmodernism: The Victorian Tradition and the Contemporary British Novel,* Rodopi, 2001
> A thorough study of postmodernism and retro-Victorian fiction from the 1960s to 2000

Linda Hutcheon, *A Poetics of Postmodernism: History, Theory, Fiction*, Routledge, 1988
> Good introduction on postmodernism from a critic who has many insights into John Fowles

Frederick P. W. McDowell, 'Recent British Fiction: Some Established Writers' in *Contemporary Literature* 11, No. 3, 1970
> Useful section on Fowles along with other twentieth-century novelists

Barbara McKenzie, *The Process of Fiction*, Harcourt, Brace, 1969
Useful for comments on narrative method and intervention of the narrator

Neil McEwan, *The Survival of the Novel: British Fiction in the Later Twentieth Century*, Macmillan, 1983
A section on John Fowles in the light of experimental attitudes to fiction

John Sutherland, *Victorian Fiction: Writers, Publishers, Readers*, Macmillan, 1995
References to five major novelists alongside fascinating consideration of others, popular in their day but now out of fashion; examines the role of publishers, and the Victorian public's demand for fiction

Claire Tomalin, *Thomas Hardy: The Time-Torn Man*, Penguin, 2007
Excellent readable biography to complement Hardy references in Fowles's writings

Patricia Waugh, ed., *Postmodernism*, Edward Arnold, 1992
A collection of essays tracing the development of postmodernism, placing it in context historically and in relation to modern literary criticism

SELECT CRITICAL WORKS ON JOHN FOWLES

James R. Aubrey, *John Fowles: A Reference Companion*, Greenwood, 1991
A useful biographical section; notes on Fowles's non-fictional writings and the main novels, with a section that surveys critical approaches up to 1990

James Aubrey, ed., *John Fowles and Nature*, Associated University Presses, 1999
A collection of fourteen essays on Fowles by major critics, a useful introduction by Aubrey and an 'Afterword' by John Fowles. See especially Carol M. Barnum, 'The Nature of John Fowles'; Suzanne Ross, '"Water out of a Woodland Spring": Sarah Woodruff and Nature in *The French Lieutenant's Woman*'; and Eileen Warburton, 'The Corpse in the Combe: The Vision of the Dead Woman in the Landscapes of John Fowles'

Carol M. Barnum *The Fiction of John Fowles*, Penkevill, 1988
Useful introduction with reference to Jung and Fowles's protagonists; full chapter of analysis on *The French Lieutenant's Woman*

Peter Conradi, *John Fowles*, Contemporary Writers series, Methuen, 1982
Relates Fowles's work to his life and to various literary genres

Pamela Cooper, *The Fictions of John Fowles: Power, Creativity, Femininity*, University of Ottawa, 1991
Looks at gender and power and the theme of freedom from a feminist, postmodernist perspective

H. W. Fawkner, *The Timescapes of John Fowles*, Fairleigh Dickinson UP, 1984
Explores the idea of temporality and essential themes in the novels of Fowles

Thomas C. Foster, *Understanding John Fowles*, University of South Carolina, 1994
Good overview in section 'Men, Women and Novels'; full chapter on *The French Lieutenant's Woman*

Robert Huffaker, *John Fowles*, Twayne, 1980
A full chapter on *The French Lieutenant's Woman* in seven sections, dealing with the main aspects of the book

Tony E. Jackson, 'Charles and the Hopeful Monster: Postmodern Evolutionary Theory in *The French Lieutenant's Woman*', in *Twentieth Century Literature* 43:2, Summer, 1979

David Landrum, 'Rewriting Marx: Emancipation and Restoration in *The French Lieutenant's Woman*', in *Mosaic* 33.1, March, 2000 (pp. 103–13)

Simon Loveday, *The Romances of John Fowles*, Macmillan, 1985
Traces romance and realism and the idea of the romantic quest in Fowles's novels

Barry N. Olshen, *John Fowles*, Frederick Ungar, 1978
A full chapter of analysis on each of the novels from *The Collector* to *Daniel Martin*

Ellen Pifer, ed., *Critical Essays on John Fowles*, G. K. Hall, 1986
A collection of essays from academic experts on Fowles, including Linda Hutcheon, 'The "Real World(s)" of Fiction: *The French Lieutenant's Woman*', and one by Fowles himself

Elizabeth Rankin, 'Cryptic Coloration in *The French Lieutenant's Woman*', in *Journal of Narrative Technique* 3, 1973 (pp. 193–207)

Mahmoud Salami, *John Fowles's Fiction and the Poetics of Postmodernism*, Associated University Presses, 1992
An introductory chapter on literary theory and the fiction of John Fowles and a full chapter on *The French Lieutenant's Woman*, concentrating on history, ideology and intertextuality

William Stephenson, *John Fowles*, Northcote House, 2003
Divides Fowles's work into three periods, the middle period 1966–79 being the most relevant for *The French Lieutenant's Woman*

Katherine Tarbox, *The Art of John Fowles*, University of Georgia Press, 1988
A full chapter on *The French Lieutenant's Woman* and an interview with Fowles

Eileen Warburton, *John Fowles: A Life in Two Worlds*, Cape, 2004
Readable and detailed biography; insight into Fowles's life and work with detail from many sources including Fowles's diaries

Peter Wolfe, *John Fowles: Magus and Moralist*, Associated University Presses, 1979
Chapter 4, 'Iron Law and the Golden Age', offers a thorough analysis of *The French Lieutenant's Woman*

Bruce Woodcock, *Male Mythologies: John Fowles and Masculinity*, Barnes, 1984
Looks at Fowles's main male characters as patriarchal figures and their ambiguities in the exploration of the idea of sexual myths

alienation a distancing effect – the term defines attempts by the artist to prevent the reader from identifying with or trusting what is taking place in a text (or play, or film); the reader (or viewer) is led to be a more critical observer

allegory (allegorise) a narrative with two levels of meaning, the straightforward, literal meaning representing a deeper meaning beneath the surface.

allusion a reference to another work of literature, historical fact, art form or biographical detail, intended to add further meaning to a text

ambiguity (ambiguous) the capacity of words to have double, multiple or uncertain meanings

anachronism something belonging to a period other than the one in which it exists

dénouement the unfolding or unravelling of a plot or story

dialect form of speech used in a particular region or class

Gothic in literature or art, a form of Romanticism that deals with passionate, horrific, mysterious, sexual or supernatural elements. It often employs medieval settings or atmosphere and was popular in the late eighteenth and nineteenth centuries

iconography the use of subjects, objects and symbols in painting, and also the study of such features

imagery descriptive language which uses images to make actions, objects and characters more vivid in the reader's mind

intertextuality a term that suggests texts do not exist alone but have relationships with other texts that enhance meaning; a writer may deliberately introduce material from other texts for this effect

irony saying or writing one thing but implying another; a situation where words are given meanings other than the literal or intended one. Irony, therefore, may be intended or unconscious

ludic subversion the playful (from the Latin *ludus*, 'game') association of realism with postmodern devices in order to challenge the reader's expectations; a form of parody

Marxism (Marxist) a political theory (and subsequently a literary critical approach) evolving from the writings of Karl Marx and Friedrich Engels that has the ideas of capitalism, class and social change as its central concerns

melodrama (melodramatic) a text, or passage of narrative, in which extravagance, sensation and elements of violence, evil or sexuality may appear

metafiction, metanarrative a narrative that is aware of its own status as a construct, possibly even commenting upon it; often used as a frame for more traditional narrative

modernism a cultural and artistic movement of the late nineteenth and early twentieth centuries involving experimentation and a reaction against earlier traditions of style, form or expression

motif a recurring idea or image in a text that draws attention to a theme or topic

narrative a story, tale or any recital of events, and the manner in which it is told

parody the copying of another style with a comic or playful discrepancy between the two texts

pastiche copying the style of another text; a more neutral form than **parody**

pathetic fallacy the transference of human emotions to inanimate objects or natural phenomena

postmodernism a term that embraces other forms of criticism, notably feminism, Marxism, existentialism and psychoanalytic criticism. As a literary movement, it devolves from the threats to mankind of the mid and late twentieth century, reflecting the doubts and fears of the period

poststructuralism a theory that suggests that the meaning of words is not absolute but varies with the context in which they are used

satire a type of writing in which ideas or issues are held up to derision or amusement through ridicule, **irony**, **parody** or exaggeration

subtext the underlying theme in a text, whose meaning is not directly stated but can be inferred

symbolism the investing of material objects with abstract meanings beyond their own; often permits a complex idea to be represented by a concrete image

trope a figure of speech in which language is used in other than a literal sense, usually in a metaphoric or **ironic** sense

voice the persona(e) created by a writer to tell the story; may include the persona of an overt narrator and even the voice of the author in the text

AUTHOR OF THESE NOTES

Michael Duffy is a former English teacher with thirty-eight years' experience, having taught in both Canada and the UK. He has a degree from De La Salle College, University of Manchester, and was head of English at St Mary's College, Blackpool, for twenty-five years. He is a published writer and the author of the York Notes Advanced title on Angela Carter's *Wise Children*. He has also worked as a senior examiner.

GCSE

Maya Angelou
I Know Why the Caged Bird Sings

Jane Austen
Pride and Prejudice

Alan Ayckbourn
Absent Friends

Elizabeth Barrett Browning
Selected Poems

Robert Bolt
A Man for All Seasons

Harold Brighouse
Hobson's Choice

Charlotte Brontë
Jane Eyre

Emily Brontë
Wuthering Heights

Brian Clark
Whose Life is it Anyway?

Robert Cormier
Heroes

Shelagh Delaney
A Taste of Honey

Charles Dickens
David Copperfield
Great Expectations
Hard Times
Oliver Twist
Selected Stories

Roddy Doyle
Paddy Clarke Ha Ha Ha

George Eliot
Silas Marner
The Mill on the Floss

Anne Frank
The Diary of a Young Girl

William Golding
Lord of the Flies

Oliver Goldsmith
She Stoops to Conquer

Willis Hall
The Long and the Short and the Tall

Thomas Hardy
Far from the Madding Crowd
The Mayor of Casterbridge
Tess of the d'Urbervilles
The Withered Arm and other Wessex Tales

L. P. Hartley
The Go-Between

Seamus Heaney
Selected Poems

Susan Hill
I'm the King of the Castle

Barry Hines
A Kestrel for a Knave

Louise Lawrence
Children of the Dust

Harper Lee
To Kill a Mockingbird

Laurie Lee
Cider with Rosie

Arthur Miller
The Crucible
A View from the Bridge

Robert O'Brien
Z for Zachariah

Frank O'Connor
My Oedipus Complex and Other Stories

George Orwell
Animal Farm

J. B. Priestley
An Inspector Calls
When We Are Married

Willy Russell
Educating Rita
Our Day Out

J. D. Salinger
The Catcher in the Rye

William Shakespeare
Henry IV Part I
Henry V
Julius Caesar
Macbeth
The Merchant of Venice
A Midsummer Night's Dream
Much Ado About Nothing
Romeo and Juliet
The Tempest
Twelfth Night

George Bernard Shaw
Pygmalion

Mary Shelley
Frankenstein

R. C. Sherriff
Journey's End

Rukshana Smith
Salt on the Snow

John Steinbeck
Of Mice and Men

Robert Louis Stevenson
Dr Jekyll and Mr Hyde

Jonathan Swift
Gulliver's Travels

Robert Swindells
Daz 4 Zoe

Mildred D. Taylor
Roll of Thunder, Hear My Cry

Mark Twain
Huckleberry Finn

James Watson
Talking in Whispers

Edith Wharton
Ethan Frome

William Wordsworth
Selected Poems

A Choice of Poets

Mystery Stories of the Nineteenth Century including The Signalman

Nineteenth Century Short Stories

Poetry of the First World War

Six Women Poets

For the AQA Anthology:

Duffy and Armitage & Pre-1914 Poetry

Heaney and Clarke & Pre-1914 Poetry

Poems from Different Cultures

Key Stage 3

William Shakespeare
Much Ado About Nothing
Richard III
The Tempest

Margaret Atwood
Cat's Eye
The Handmaid's Tale

Jane Austen
Emma
Mansfield Park
Persuasion
Pride and Prejudice
Sense and Sensibility

Pat Barker
Regeneration

William Blake
Songs of Innocence and of Experience

The Brontës
Selected Poems

Charlotte Brontë
Jane Eyre
Villette

Emily Brontë
Wuthering Heights

Angela Carter
The Bloody Chamber
Nights at the Circus
Wise Children

Geoffrey Chaucer
The Franklin's Prologue and Tale
The Merchant's Prologue and Tale
The Miller's Prologue and Tale
The Prologue to the Canterbury Tales
The Pardoner's Tale
The Wife of Bath's Prologue and Tale

Caryl Churchill
Top Girls

John Clare
Selected Poems

Joseph Conrad
Heart of Darkness

Charles Dickens
Bleak House
Great Expectations
Hard Times

John Donne
Selected Poems

Carol Ann Duffy
Selected Poems
The World's Wife

George Eliot
Middlemarch
The Mill on the Floss

T. S. Eliot
Selected Poems
The Waste Land

Sebastian Faulks
Birdsong

F. Scott Fitzgerald
The Great Gatsby

John Ford
'Tis Pity She's a Whore

John Fowles
The French Lieutenant's Woman

Michael Frayn
Spies

Charles Frazier
Cold Mountain

Brian Friel
Making History
Translations

William Golding
The Spire

Thomas Hardy
Jude the Obscure
The Mayor of Casterbridge
The Return of the Native
Selected Poems
Tess of the d'Urbervilles

Nathaniel Hawthorne
The Scarlet Letter

Seamus Heaney
Selected Poems from 'Opened Ground'

Homer
The Iliad
The Odyssey

Khaled Hosseini
The Kite Runner

Aldous Huxley
Brave New World

Henrik Ibsen
A Doll's House

James Joyce
Dubliners

John Keats
Selected Poems

Philip Larkin
High Windows
The Whitsun Weddings and Selected Poems

Ian McEwan
Atonement

Christopher Marlowe
Doctor Faustus
Edward II

Arthur Miller
All My Sons
Death of a Salesman

John Milton
Paradise Lost Books I and II

George Orwell
Nineteen Eighty-Four

Sylvia Plath
Selected Poems

William Shakespeare
Antony and Cleopatra
As You Like It
Hamlet
Henry IV Part I
King Lear
Macbeth
Measure for Measure
The Merchant of Venice
A Midsummer Night's Dream
Much Ado About Nothing
Othello
Richard II
Richard III
Romeo and Juliet
The Taming of the Shrew
The Tempest
Twelfth Night
The Winter's Tale

Mary Shelley
Frankenstein

Richard Brinsley Sheridan
The School for Scandal

Bram Stoker
Dracula

Alfred Tennyson
Selected Poems

Virgil
The Aeneid

Alice Walker
The Color Purple

John Webster
The Duchess of Malfi
The White Devil

Oscar Wilde
The Importance of Being Earnest
The Picture of Dorian Gray
A Woman of No Importance

Tennessee Williams
Cat on a Hot Tin Roof
The Glass Menagerie
A Streetcar Named Desire

Jeanette Winterson
Oranges Are Not the Only Fruit

Virginia Woolf
To the Lighthouse

William Wordsworth
The Prelude and Selected Poems

Wordsworth and Coleridge
Lyrical Ballads

Poetry of the First World War